SpringerBriefs in Law

SpringerBriefs present concise summaries of cutting-edge research and practical applications across a wide spectrum of fields. Featuring compact volumes of 50 to 125 pages, the series covers a range of content from professional to academic. Typical topics might include:

- A timely report of state-of-the art analytical techniques
- A bridge between new research results, as published in journal articles, and a contextual literature review
- A snapshot of a hot or emerging topic
- A presentation of core concepts that students must understand in order to make independent contributions

SpringerBriefs in Law showcase emerging theory, empirical research, and practical application in Law from a global author community. SpringerBriefs are characterized by fast, global electronic dissemination, standard publishing contracts, standardized manuscript preparation and formatting guidelines, and expedited production schedules.

Erich Vranes

WTO Security Exceptions in Practice and Scholarship

Curtailing "Trump Cards" through Proportionality

Springer

Erich Vranes
Institute for European and International Law
Vienna University of Economics and
Business (WU Wien)
Vienna, Austria

ISSN 2192-855X ISSN 2192-8568 (electronic)
SpringerBriefs in Law
ISBN 978-3-031-36701-4 ISBN 978-3-031-36702-1 (eBook)
https://doi.org/10.1007/978-3-031-36702-1

This Springer imprint is published by the registered company Springer Nature Switzerland AG
The registered company address is: Gewerbestrasse 11, 6330 Cham, Switzerland

Preface

For many decades, the security exceptions in GATT/WTO law have been regarded as the “boxes of Pandora” of the WTO regime. This is due to their alleged self-judging character, which has been understood, by several WTO Members and academics, as making it possible for a WTO Member to escape its obligations under WTO law by merely invoking these clauses when it claims that its national security is at stake.

Due to the potentially vast effects of the security exceptions for the functioning of the world trading system, the Members of the WTO and the Contracting Parties of the GATT 1947 had usually tried to avoid panel proceedings in cases involving security issues. Against this background, the recent invocation of these exceptions in WTO trade disputes has rightly been regarded as the turn of an era.

The present contribution first explains the political and geopolitical background of the increasing importance of security exceptions in the WTO regime and international economic law more generally. It also provides an analysis of how these exceptions have been interpreted and applied in the seminal landmark WTO panel reports *Russia – Transit*, *Saudi Arabia – IPRs* and *US Steel*, which were issued between 2019 and December 2022. This study furthermore addresses theoretical and methodological aspects relating to the interpretation of the WTO security exceptions, arguing that these alleged “trump cards” should be reviewed, or “curtailed”, in particular through a proportionality analysis.

This study is part of a series of projects concluded during a sabbatical semester at the Vienna University of Economics and Business (WU Wien). I would like to express my gratitude to WU Wien for this welcome support. I am also grateful to the editors of the *Springer Briefs in Law* Series for accepting this contribution and their smooth and effective management of the review and publication process as well as to Sophie Bohnert, LL.M. (WU), BSc (WU), for very helpful research assistance.

Vienna, Austria
May 2023

Erich Vranes

Contents

Chapter 1
Introduction: The "Sleeping Dragon" of WTO Law

In 2019, the "sleeping dragon"[1] of WTO law was awakened. The "sleeping dragon" or "sleeping dog"[2] in this context is Article XXI, the security exception of the GATT, which has been successfully invoked by Russia in a high-profile WTO dispute against Ukraine, the *Russia – Transit* case.[3] In 2020, the central findings of this landmark ruling were largely confirmed in a second closely watched dispute dealing with trade measures imposed by Saudi Arabia against Qatar (*Saudi Arabia – IPRs*).[4] Like Russia, Saudi Arabia had claimed that these measures were required for national security reasons. A series of further proceedings have been triggered meanwhile,[5] which have resulted in four panel reports in the *US – Steel* dispute, which were circulated to the Members of the WTO in December 2022.[6]

---

[1] Paulsen (2022).

[2] Mantilla Blanco and Pehl (2020), p. 5.

[3] WTO panel report, *Russia – Measures Concerning Traffic in Transit*, WT/DS512/R and Add.1, adopted 26 April 2019, DSR 2019:VIII, 4301 (in the following: *Russia – Transit*).

[4] WTO panel report, *Saudi Arabia – Measures Concerning the Protection of Intellectual Property Rights*, WT/DS567/R and Add.1, circulated to WTO Members on 16 June 2020 (in the following: *Saudi Arabia – IPRs*). This dispute has been terminated while the appeal to the WTO Appellate Body was pending and has not become binding, therefore. However, it is expected that this panel report will remain influential; on this see below, Sect. 3.2.

[5] According to Van den Bossche and Akpofure (2020), the WTO security exceptions have been invoked in seven disputes; according to Vidigal (2019), p. 25, the interpretation in *Russia – Transit* impacts 23 WTO disputes that were pending in 2019.

[6] These are the reports in the proceedings triggered by China, Norway, Switzerland and Turkey (*United States – Certain Measures on Steel and Aluminium Products*, WT/DS544/R, Add.1 and Suppl.1, circulated to WTO Members 9 December 2022 (*US – Steel (China)), United States – Certain Measures on Steel and Aluminium Products*, WT/DS552/R, Add.1 and Suppl.1, circulated to WTO Members 9 December 2022 (*US – Steel (Norway), United States – Certain Measures on Steel and Aluminium Products*, WT/DS556/R, Add.1 and Suppl.1, circulated to WTO Members 9 December 2022 (*US – Steel (Switzerland)), United States – Certain Measures on Steel and Aluminium Products*, WT/DS564/R, Add.1 and Suppl.1, circulated to WTO Members 9 December

E. Vranes, *WTO Security Exceptions in Practice and Scholarship*, SpringerBriefs in Law, https://doi.org/10.1007/978-3-031-36702-1_1

The reason why Article XXI of the GATT is regarded as being a principal, but eminently problematical provision of WTO law is that it has often been regarded as possessing a "self-judging" character: According to one rigorous view, which is often entertained, the invocation of Article XXI should automatically oust a WTO panel's jurisdiction in cases involving national security issues. In this vein, it has been submitted for example that Article XXI is an "unreviewable trump card" that functions as an "exception to all WTO rules that can be exercised at the sole discretion of a Member State", thereby providing WTO Members with an "unaccountable sovereign domain".[7] According to more moderate views, invoking this provision would require WTO panels to reduce their degree of scrutiny under relevant criteria set forth in this cardinal provision.[8] Due to the first view, which has prominently been held e.g. by the US,[9] Article XXI of the GATT has also been called the "box of Pandora" of WTO law[10] and the "Sword of Damocles" pending over the WTO regime.[11]

As has been submitted, invoking Article XXI—or the analogously worded security exceptions in the GATS and TRIPS Agreements[12]—may lead to a lose-lose situation: If a panel were to rule that it does not have jurisdiction when a respondent relies on this provision, then other WTO Members could do so, too, in future cases.[13] By contrast, if a ruling subjects these security exceptions to limitations, this could be seen by some WTO Members as a breach of state sovereignty, raising the spectre of WTO Members ignoring such rulings or even withdrawing from the WTO.[14] The fact that this risk is real is borne out by a threat of the US, issued in a meeting of the WTO Dispute Settlement Body, which addressed the *US – Steel* dispute.[15] In this meeting the US cautioned that "if the WTO were to undertake to review an invocation of Article XXI, this would undermine the legitimacy of the WTO's dispute settlement system and even the viability of the WTO as a whole".[16]

2022 (*US – Steel (Turkey)*). Proceedings started by other WTO Members have been terminated or are still pending (see below, Sect. 3.6).

[7] Alford (2011), pp. 698–699; see e.g. also Bhala (1998), p. 268 (claiming that no panel has jurisdiction over Article XXI of the GATT).

[8] See e.g. Schill and Briese (2009), p. 66.

[9] On the US position see e.g. the panel report, *Russia – Transit*, paras 7.51–52; on this see also Van den Bossche and Akpofure (2020), text at fn 26.

[10] Roberts et al. (2019); Boklan and Bahri (2020), p. 123; Van den Bossche and Akpofure (2020), text at fn 21.

[11] Milanov (2021), pp. 551–552.

[12] Article XIV*bis* of the GATS and Article 73 of the TRIPS; on these provisions see below, Sect. 3.3.

[13] Reinsch and Caporal (2019).

[14] Reinsch and Caporal (2019).

[15] On this dispute see below, Sect. 3.6.

[16] Cf WTO, Minutes of the DSB Meeting, WTO document WT/DSB/M/421 of 2 April 2019, para 7.2.; on this cf. also Van den Bossche and Akpofure (2020), text at fn 32.

A similar warning had been pronounced by Russia in the course of the *Russia – Transit* proceedings.[17]

In brief, these stances reflect conflicting views of the world trade regime: whereas several commentators argue that the WTO system would collapse, if panels were to decline jurisdiction in trade disputes potentially involving security issues,[18] the US and others conversely claim that exercising jurisdiction in such cases might spell the end of the WTO.

Indeed, the mere invocation of Article XXI in the aforementioned panel proceedings has been said to constitute the turn of an era, given that WTO Members and before them the Contracting Parties of the GATT 1947 had usually tried to find alternatives to such procedures when security issues were at stake.[19] In view of long-standing debates in state practice and academic writings on whether Article XXI is fully "self-judging" in the sense of barring the competence of WTO panels, it is of systemic importance that the reports in *Russia – Transit* and *Saudi Arabia – IPRs* as well as the 2022 reports in *US – Steel* have clarified that WTO panels indeed have jurisdiction over trade disputes possessing national security dimensions.[20]

It is expected, therefore, that academic discussions will now turn to the question of the appropriate degree of deference panels should pay to WTO Members trying to justify trade restrictions by relying on the security exceptions in the WTO agreements.[21] In fact, a great number of case notes and analyses of this issue have been published meanwhile.[22] However, an argument made be *Schill* and *Briese* in a seminal analysis of self-judging clauses in general, and security exceptions in particular, still holds true today, namely that the interpretation and application of such clauses appears "undertheorized".[23]

This contribution will focus on Article XXI(b)(iii) of the GATT (and the analogous provisions of Article XIV*bis*(1)(b)(iii) of the GATS and Article 73(b)(iii) of the TRIPS Agreements), which, being concerned with emergencies in international relations, has the most practical and systemic relevance and has also influenced the wording of a considerable number of trade and investment agreements as well as several rulings outside the WTO framework. A central problem in this context are the aforementioned apparently irreconcilable views that exercising jurisdiction in security-related trade disputes risks affecting the legitimacy, or even existence, of the WTO, whereas declining jurisdiction in such cases may likewise undermine the

[17] Panel report, *Russia – Transit*, para 7.22 ("Russia cautions that involving the WTO in political and security matters will upset the very delicate balance of rights and obligations under the WTO Agreements and endanger the multilateral trading system").

[18] See e.g. Schloemann and Ohlhoff (1999), pp. 426 ff.

[19] Cf e.g. Glöckle (2020); Heath (2020), pp. 1024 ff.

[20] Gladysz (2021), pp. 848 ff; Vidigal (2019), p. 223.

[21] Van den Bossche and Akpofure (2020).

[22] See e.g. Bogdanova (2021), pp. 171 ff; Boklan and Bahri (2020), pp. 123 ff; Cohen (2020), pp. 793 ff; Gladysz (2021), pp. 835 ff; Glöckle (2020); Milanov (2021), pp. 547 ff.

[23] Schill and Briese (2009), p. 65.

WTO dispute settlement system. Panels dealing with such disputes therefore have to walk a tightrope.[24] A vital task here is finding an adequate balance of WTO rights and obligations. This is where adequate theory is needed most.

The present contribution will therefore proceed as follows: After an explanation of the political and geopolitical background of the increasing importance of the WTO security exceptions in Chap. 2, it will analyse how these exceptions have been interpreted and applied in the aforementioned seminal panel reports (Chap. 3), and will finally address theoretical and methodological aspects relating to the interpretation of these exceptions in Chap. 4, where it will also be argued that these alleged "trump cards" should be reviewed, or "curtailed", in particular through a proportionality analysis that encompasses the assessment of the suitability and necessity of the measures employed by a WTO Member invoking the WTO security exceptions.

References

Alford RR (2011) The self-judging WTO security exception. Utah Law Rev 3:697–759

Bhala R (1998) National security and international trade law. Univ Pa J Int Law 19(2):263–317

Bogdanova I (2021) Targeted economic sanctions and WTO law. Leg Issues Econ Integr 48(2): 171–200

Boklan D, Bahri A (2020) The first WTO's ruling on national security exception. World Trade Rev 19:123–136

Cohen HG (2020) Nations and markets. J Int Econ Law 23:793–815

Gladysz J (2021) The national security exception in WTO law: emerging jurisprudence and future direction. Georgetown J Int Law 52:835–861

Glöckle C (2020) The second chapter on a national security exception in WTO law. EJIL Talk, 22 July 2020. https://www.ejiltalk.org/the-second-chapter-on-a-national-security-exception-in-wto-law-the-panel-report-in-saudi-arabia-protection-of-ipr. Accessed 4 Jan 2023

Heath JB (2020) The new national security challenge to the economic order. Yale Law J 129:1020–1098

Mantilla Blanco S, Pehl A (2020) National security exceptions in international trade and investment agreements. Justiciability and standards of review. Springer, Cham

Milanov M (2021) A Lauterpachtian affair: security exceptions as 'self-judging obligations' in the case law of the International Court of Justice and beyond. J World Invest Trade 22:509–560

Paulsen M (2022) Characterizing war in a trade context. Opinio Juris, 10 March 2022. https://opiniojuris.org/2022/03/10/characterizing-war-in-a-trade-context. Accessed 4 Jan 2023

Reinsch WA, Caporal J (2019) The WTO's first ruling on national security. Center for Strategic and International Studies, 5 April 2019. https://www.csis.org/analysis/wtos-first-ruling-national-security-what-does-it-mean-united-states. Accessed 4 Jan 2023

Roberts A, Choer Moraes H, Ferguson V (2019) Toward a geoeconomic order in international trade and investment. J Int Econ Law 22:655–676

Schill S, Briese R (2009) "If the state considers": self-judging clauses in international dispute settlement. In: von Bogdandy A, Wolfrum R (eds) Max Planck Yearbook of United Nations Law, vol 13, pp 61–140

Schloemann HL, Ohlhoff S (1999) Constitutionalization and dispute settlement in the WTO: national security as an issue of competence. Am J Int Law 93:424–451

[24] Milanov (2021), p. 515.

Van den Bossche PL, Akpofure S (2020) The use and abuse of the national security exception under article XXI(b)(iii) of the GATT 1994. WTI Working Paper No. 03/2020. https://www.wti.org/research/publications/1299/the-use-and-abuse-of-the-national-securityexception-under-article-xxibiii-of-the-gatt-1994. Accessed 4 January 2023

Vidigal G (2019) WTO adjudication and the security exception: something old, something new, something borrowed – something blue? Leg Issues Econ Integr 46(3):203–224

Chapter 2
(Geo-)Political Background: From Interdependence to "Permanent Exceptionalism"?

Security exceptions in international trade and investment agreements are pivotal for the interplay between politics and law in international relations.[1] This is because the concepts of jurisdiction and deference—which, as indicated, are closely associated with security exceptions—are formative for the role played by tribunals vis-à-vis states. If such clauses were regarded as "totally self-judging",[2] then they would amount to "vanishing points of international law" in a Lauterpachtian sense.[3] However, this arguably is precisely why states, typically for reasons of short-term self-interest, increasingly tend to invoke security exceptions, claiming that international courts or tribunals have no jurisdiction (or must at least apply a considerably reduced degree of scrutiny) in cases allegedly involving security issues, in order to free themselves from international obligations and gain room of manoeuvre. As has been noted, there seem to be few cases where respondent states have not claimed that the security exception at issue is "self-judging".[4]

Yet, security exceptions are not only determinant for the interaction between international tribunals and politics. They also play a primary role in the current transformation of the international economic order, which is driven above all by the struggle for economic and political predominance on a global level.[5] This struggle evidently extends far beyond trade relations in that it constitutes a competition

---

[1] Milanov (2021), p. 513.

[2] As had been submitted by Russia in *Russia – Transit*, para 7.26; on this see below, Sect. 3.1.

[3] On this cf. in particular Milanov (2021), p. 520.

[4] Milanov (2021), p. 521. The practical relevance of possible invocations of the security exceptions is considerable: Thus, the US was said to have imposed trade sanctions against 90 countries in one 10-year period (Alford 2011, p. 700). Moreover, after the Russian invasion of Ukraine in 2022, several states have suspended the most-favoured nation status of Russia. In this context, Article XXI of the GATT is again seen as the relevant clause for justifying such measures (cf. Collins 2022).

[5] On this transformation of the international economic order cf. e.g. Reinecke (2019), pp. 1 ff; Fischer (2019), pp. 8 ff; Slawotsky (2021), pp. 545 ff.

E. Vranes, *WTO Security Exceptions in Practice and Scholarship*, SpringerBriefs in Law, https://doi.org/10.1007/978-3-031-36702-1_2

between rival political and economic systems,[6] in which in particular China and the US tend to resort to unusual means.[7] Nonetheless, trade measures are used as primary instruments of "economic statecraft"[8] in this struggle and are perceived as being "weaponized" for broader strategic goals.[9] It is obvious that states using such measures come under an increased need for justification, which is why security exceptions, as the "ultimate means of justification",[10] become more important in today's era of geoeconomics.[11]

This development goes hand in hand with, and reinforces, a second current trend, namely attempts to expand the concept of "national security" and apply it to additional and new concerns. Thus, apprehensions relating to data and cyber-security, critical infrastructure, terrorism, economic crises, human trafficking, contagious diseases, climate change and others are increasingly discussed under the keyword of "national security".[12] On the level of political aims we are thus witnessing a "securitization"[13] of an increasing range of interests; on the level of the means employed, a "weaponization of trade instruments" is taking place.

It is expected that the struggle for global predominance and the reordering of the international economic order will remain a long-standing conflict,[14] not least because many players seem to have gained the impression that economic interdependency equals undesirable dependency.[15] This indeed constitutes a partial change of paradigms: On the one hand, according to classic economic theory, international trade creates a win-win situation, an assumption which had spurred an increasing legalization of the international trading regime (including the establishment of international dispute settlement mechanisms like that of the WTO in 1995 and a growing consensus that trade relations should be governed by law rather than diplomacy) and had inter alia resulted in at least partially shielding the trade

---

[6] Cf e.g. Fischer (2019), pp. 8 ff.

[7] Thus, the US on the one hand uses ideological response measures, technical boycotts, attempts at economic decoupling from other countries like China in particular, and visa restrictions e.g. in the academic and strategic research arena (cf. e.g. Gu 2019, p. 15). China, on the other hand, has started projects such as the "Belt and Road Initiative", large-scale investments in industrialized and developing countries supported by the Chinese government, and the "Made in China 2025" strategy (cf. e.g. Reinecke (2019), pp. 5 ff).

[8] "Statecraft" has been defined as the use of policy instruments (such as military, economic, diplomatic and informational measures) to attain multiple objectives, such as promoting security, prosperity and influence. "Economic statecraft" in this context can be understood as the use of trade and economic measures more generally to promote such goals. On this cf. Mastanduno (1998), pp. 825 ff.

[9] Bhala (1998), pp. 263 ff; Zhou (2020).

[10] Mantilla Blanco and Pehl (2020), p. 1.

[11] Cohen (2020), pp. 793 ff.

[12] Cohen (2020), pp. 805–806; Gladysz (2021), p. 836, fn 1; Slawotsky (2021), pp. 545 ff.

[13] Gladysz (2021), p. 836, fn 1.

[14] Roberts et al. (2019), p. 655; Slawotsky (2021), pp. 545 ff; Oermann and Wolff (2019), pp. 12 ff.

[15] Oermann and Wolff (2019), pp. 12 ff.

regime from world politics.[16] This development had also been nourished by the widely held view that economic interdependence leads to peace,[17] perhaps most succinctly summed up in the quote "if goods don't cross frontiers, soldiers will".[18]

Today, on the other hand, interdependence is increasingly perceived as strategic vulnerability.[19] This impression has also provoked a partial "return of the past",[20] in that states reintroduce measures aiming to protect their national industry, a trend that has resulted in the Trump administration's declaration that "economic security is national security".[21] This tendency could be further reinforced by states feeling the need to take measures to mend their national economies after the Covid pandemic.[22] The idea that economic self-sufficiency should be promoted is also gaining ground due the strategy of some crucial players in the world economy that are said to "weaponize interdependence" by exploiting the weaker status of dependent partner states,[23] which has already led to trade disputes in the WTO framework.[24] Moreover, as has rightly been submitted, in a globalized world with complex supply chains any key products could be seen, or used, as a source of such "weaponized interdependence".[25]

As has also been noted, these trends risk leading to a state of "permanent exceptionalism",[26] where national security clauses are routinely invoked with the result that the exceptions might "swallow the rule".[27] Since further cases in which security exceptions like Article XXI of the GATT will be relied on are expected,[28] there also is an increasing danger of abuse of these clauses. Moreover, in the light of the developments just outlined, security exceptions are not merely seen as "escape valves" in crises of a predominantly military character as in the past,[29] but

[16] See Roberts et al. (2019), pp. 657 ff.

[17] Hahn (1991), p. 581.

[18] Boklan and Bahri (2020), p. 124, fn 3, referring to a citation attributed to the French economist Frédéric Bastiat.

[19] See e.g. Weiß (2020), p. 831.

[20] As noted by Heath (2020b), pp. 229 ff (quotation at p. 229).

[21] Heath (2020b), pp. 229 ff with further references.

[22] Arato et al. (2020), p. 633.

[23] Roberts et al. (2019), pp. 659 ff, referring to Chinese measures such as the "Belt and Road Initiative", the creation of alternatives to the SWIFT banking system and an alternative Chinese internet.

[24] An ominous case in point is a trade dispute between Japan and South Korea over semiconductors; on this cf. Zhou (2020).

[25] Cohen (2020), p. 806.

[26] Arato et al. (2020), pp. 627 ff and 633; Roberts et al. (2019), p. 655; see also Heath (2020a), pp. 1032 ff.

[27] Roberts et al. (2019), p. 665.

[28] Gladysz (2021), p. 842.

[29] Schill and Briese (2009), p. 67; Mantilla Blanco and Pehl (2020), pp. 1 ff.

increasingly also as tools for recalibrating trade and substantially more broadly conceived security concerns.[30]

All of this calls for an in-depth analysis of the functioning of the WTO security exceptions in the light of the recent WTO panel reports mentioned.

References

Alford RR (2011) The self-judging WTO security exception. Utah Law Rev 3:697–759

Arato J, Claussen K, Heath B (2020) The perils of pandemic exceptionalism. Am J Int Law 114(4): 627–636

Bhala R (1998) National security and international trade law. Univ Pa J Int Law 19(2):263–317

Boklan D, Bahri A (2020) The first WTO's ruling on national security exception. World Trade Rev 19:123–136

Cohen HG (2020) Nations and markets. J Int Econ Law 23:793–815

Collins D (2022) The WTO's essential security exception and revocation of Russia's most favoured nation status following the invasion of Ukraine. *City Law Forum*, 15 March 2022. https://blogs.city.ac.uk/citylawforum/2022/03/15/the-wtos-essentialsecurity-exception-and-revocation-of-russias-most-favoured-nation-status-following-the-invasion-of-ukraine

Fischer D (2019) Wechselnde Allianzen für verschiedene Ebenen. ifo Schnelldienst 72(22):8–11

Gladysz J (2021) The national security exception in WTO law: emerging jurisprudence and future direction. Georgetown J Int Law 52:835–861

Gu X (2019) Europas Zukunft: Äquidistanz zwischen China und Amerika. ifo Schnelldienst 72 (22):15–18. https://www.ifo.de/publikationen/2019/aufsatz-zeitschrift/die-konkurrenz-um-wirtschaftliche-dominanz-wie-kann-sich

Hahn MJ (1991) Vital interests and the law of the GATT: an analysis of GATT's security exception. Mich J Int Law 12(3):558–620

Heath JB (2020a) The new national security challenge to the economic order. Yale Law J 129:1020–1098

Heath JB (2020b) Trade and security among the ruins. Duke J Comp Int Law 30:223–266

Mantilla Blanco S, Pehl A (2020) National security exceptions in international trade and investment agreements. Justiciability and standards of review. Springer, Cham

Mastanduno M (1998) Economics and security in statecraft and scholarship. Int Organ 52(4): 825–854

Milanov M (2021) A Lauterpachtian affair: security exceptions as 'self-judging obligations' in the case law of the international court of justice and beyond. J World Invest Trade 22:509–560. https://brill.com/view/journals/jwit/22/4/articlep509_2.xml?ebody=article%20details

Oermann O, Wolff HJ (2019) Europäische Selbstwerdung und Selbstbehauptung durch wirtschaftliche Staatskunst. ifo Schnelldienst 72(22):12–15

Reinecke A (2019) Handelskonflikt oder strategische Neupositionierung? ifo Schnelldienst 72(22): 3–8

Roberts A, Choer Moraes H, Ferguson V (2019) Toward a geoeconomic order in international trade and investment. J Int Econ Law 22:655–676

Schill S, Briese R (2009) "If the state considers": self-judging clauses in international dispute settlement. In: von Bogdandy A, Wolfrum R (eds) Max Planck Yearbook of United Nations Law, vol 13, pp 61–140

[30] See also Roberts et al. (2019), pp. 659 ff.

Slawotsky J (2021) National security exception in an era of hegemonic rivalry. In: Chaisse J et al (eds) Handbook of international investment law and policy. Springer Nature, Singapore, pp 545–577

Weiß W (2020) Adjudicating security exceptions in WTO law: methodical and procedural preliminaries. J World Trade 54(6):829–852

Zhou J (2020) New WTO ruling on national security in Qatar-Saudi Arabia case and its impact on South Korea-Japan dispute. ASIL Insights 24(22), 3 September 2020. https://www.asil.org/insights/volume/24/issue/22/new-wto-ruling-national-security-qatar-saudi-arabia-case-and-its-impact. Accessed 4 Jan 2023

Chapter 3
The Security Exceptions in the GATT and TRIPS as Interpreted and Applied

This section analyses the security exceptions in the GATT (Article XXI) and the TRIPS Agreement (Article 73) in the light of the panel reports in *Russia – Transit, Saudi Arabia – IPRs* and *US – Steel,* which are the first proceedings in which the security exceptions of the GATT and TRIPS Agreement have been invoked since the entry into force of the WTO in 1995.[1] Article XXI of the GATT in particular has formed the object of long-standing debates in scholarship. The wording of Article 73 of the TRIPS Agreement is virtually identical to Article XXI of the GATT. The same holds true for Article XIV*bis* of the GATS, the GATS' security exception. Hence, the following considerations are also relevant, *mutatis mutandis*, for Article XIV*bis* of the GATS.

3.1 Terminological Clarification

For the purposes of the following analysis, it seems appropriate to point to an issue of terminology which has caused confusion in these reports and academic writings. As will be seen below, Russia as the respondent in *Russia – Transit* had claimed that Article XXI of the GATT is "totally self-judging", which has been understood by Russia and the panel as a claim that the panel does not have *jurisdiction* in cases where Article XXI is invoked.[2] On the other hand, the US, as a third party in this dispute, also argued that Article XXI is "self-judging", but understood this term as meaning that the panel possesses jurisdiction. However, according to the US, the "self-judging" nature of Article XXI would imply that its invocation is "non-justiciable" and "is therefore not capable of findings by a panel", so that it would

---

[1] State practice and panel reports in the context of the GATT 1947 are discussed in an Appendix to the Panel report, *Russia – Transit*, 106 ff.

[2] Panel report, *Russia – Transit*, para 7.26; on this see also below, Sect. 3.4.

E. Vranes, *WTO Security Exceptions in Practice and Scholarship*, SpringerBriefs in Law, https://doi.org/10.1007/978-3-031-36702-1_3

be impossible for panels to make recommendations in cases where Article XXI is at stake.[3] The US has taken a similar stance in the 2022 *US – Steel* reports, in which it claimed that the panel should restrict itself to finding that Article XXI has been invoked.[4] In *Saudi Arabia – IPRs*, by contrast, Saudi Arabia had not referred to the concepts of "jurisdiction" or "justiciability" at all, when it invoked the security exception of the TRIPS Agreement. Nonetheless, its arguments have been construed as implying that it regarded the matter in dispute as "non-justiciable". Furthermore, as noted by the panel, there seemed to be "a degree of overlap" between arguments presented by the parties and third parties in terms of "justiciability" and "jurisdiction".[5]

As can be seen from this brief overview already, the term "self-judging" does not constitute a term of art with a fixed meaning in panel practice. This impression is clearly confirmed, when one turns to academic writings in general and analyses of Article XXI of the GATT in particular. In a seminal article on "self-judging clauses", which uses Article XXI as a prime example, *Schill* and *Briese* have essentially defined such clauses as provisions which make it possible for states to escape or derogate from international obligations based on unilateral considerations.[6] However, the term "self-judging" is used with varying meanings by other authors and is regarded by some as (partially) overlapping with concepts such as "non-justiciability", "standard of review", "deference", "discretion" etc. *Schill* and *Briese*, for instance, have argued that the "self-judging" character of a norm appears to be understood in state practice and international jurisprudence as "rather" affecting the *standard of review* than as ousting a tribunal's jurisdiction.[7] Yet, this view, which refers to what these authors regard as the preponderant use of the term, as well as the term "rather" clearly imply that the term "self-judging" provisions has no definite contours and could also be used to refer to questions of jurisdiction. Indeed, *Milanov*, for example, regards the concept of "self-judging" clauses as at least partially relating to jurisdiction, as he considers the "absolutely self-judging" character of a norm as implying that this norm can be invoked as a jurisdictional defence.[8] On the other hand, according to *Milanov*, a not absolutely "self-judging" character of a provision would obviously merely imply that a tribunal must grant deference to states invoking such a clause.[9] Using the term "self-judging clauses" in a slightly deviating manner, *Mantilla Blanco* and *Pehl* apparently regard the concept of "self-judging clauses" as relating to jurisdiction, but not to the issue of the degree of deference to be accorded to WTO Members under a provision such as Article XXI.[10]

[3] Panel report, *Russia – Transit*, para 7.52.

[4] See below, Sect. 3.6.

[5] Panel report, *Saudi Arabia – IPRs*, para 7.9; on this report see also below, Sect. 3.5.

[6] Schill and Briese (2009), p. 68.

[7] Schill and Briese (2009), p. 66.

[8] Milanov (2021), p. 518.

[9] Milanov (2021), p. 521.

[10] Mantilla Blanco and Pehl (2020), p. 16.

This terminological vagueness is aggravated by authors equating the "self-judging" character of a norm with its non-justiciability,[11] whereas others do not seem to do so.[12]

In sum, it seems difficult to derive clear outlines from the various uses of the concept "self-judging". This conceptual haziness has led to a rather confusing order of analysis in the panel report in *Russia – Transit* and a deviating order of analysis in *Saudi Arabia – IPRs* and *US – Steel.*[13] Hence, as conceptual clarity is requisite, this contribution will avoid employing the terms "self-judging" and "justiciable" to the extent possible (i.e. unless it refers to relevant panel reports or authors who explicitly use these notions). Instead, it will employ the term "jurisdiction" to refer to a panel's competence to hear a case; it will use the term "inherent jurisdiction" to refer to a panel's competence to interpret the scope of its own jurisdiction;[14] and it will use the terms "deference" and "discretion accorded to a WTO Member" with respect to the standard of review employed by panels.

3.2 Order of Analysis

For the purposes of the following analysis, it seems appropriate to first address the panel report in *Russia – Transit* for several reasons: First, the structure of this report appears questionable as it arguably intermingles questions of jurisdiction, substantive assessment of a WTO Member's conduct under WTO obligations, and deference.[15] A second reason is the fact that the panel decided to address Article XXI of the GATT before determining whether Russia, as the defendant in this case, had actually violated any of its obligations under the GATT. This approach is hardly in line with the common understanding that Article XXI of the GATT functions as an affirmative defence, which has to be addressed by a WTO panel only once it has priorly been determined that the respondent WTO Member has infringed its

[11] See e.g. Milanov (2021), p. 518.

[12] Cf. Akande and Williams (2003), pp. 381 ff. Cf. also Schloemann and Ohlhoff (1999); Gladysz (2021), pp. 840–841, who submit that "non-justiciability" can assume two forms, with a strong form of non-justiciability equalling lack of jurisdiction and a weaker form of non-justiciability of a norm implying that the norm in question is subject to subjective interpretation by the state relying on it. For further views see e.g. Boklan and Bahri (2020), pp. 127 ff; Alford (2011), pp. 701 ff.

[13] See below, Sects. 3.2 and 3.4.

[14] As explained by the panel in *Russia – Transit*, one aspect of this inherent jurisdiction is the power of adjudicating bodies to determine all matters arising in relation to the exercise of their own substantive jurisdiction, which is also referred to as "*Kompetenz-Kompetenz*" in German, or "*compétence de la compétence*" in French (panel report, *Russia – Transit*, para 7.53 and fn 145 with further references).

[15] Cf. below, Sects. 3.4.2 and 3.4.3.

obligations under the GATT.[16] The reason given by the panel for its order of analysis seems debatable.[17] In contrast, the panels in *Saudi Arabia – IPRs* and *US – Steel* followed the traditional approach of first assessing whether the defendants had *prima facie* acted inconsistently with their respective obligations under the GATT or the TRIPS Agreement, before turning to the question as to whether any such infringements could be justified under the security exceptions in the GATT and the TRIPS Agreement, respectively. These divergent orders of analysis suggest that addressing these reports consecutively appears more appropriate.

Moreover, while the panel in *Saudi Arabia* claimed that it had been guided—as regards the interpretation of the substantive criteria in the security exception of the TRIPS Agreement (Article 73)—by the analytical framework set forth in the panel report in *Russia – Transit*,[18] it nonetheless seems to have deviated from this framework in several respects.[19] Furthermore, as will be seen below, the panel in *US – Steel* has adopted a self-standing approach, which differs from that of the preceding panel reports. This, too, calls for a consecutive analysis of these reports.

Finally, it should also be stressed that the panel report in *Saudi Arabia – IPRs* has not become binding, since Saudi Arabia as the defendant and Qatar as the complaining WTO Members agreed on suspending the dispute in 2021, before Qatar finally informed the WTO Dispute Settlement Body in 2022 that it would not seek adoption of the panel report.[20] Nonetheless, this report—like other

---

[16] See e.g. the EU statement in the *US – Steel* dispute: European Union, Opening Oral Statement, *United States – Certain Measures on Steel and Aluminium Products*, DS548, Geneva, 4 November 2019, para 79.

[17] In this regard, the panel argued that Article XXI(b)(iii) "acknowledges that a war or other emergency in international relations involves a *fundamental change of circumstances* which radically alters the factual matrix in which the WTO-consistency of the measures at issue is to be evaluated" and went on to state that it "considers that an evaluation of whether measures are covered by Article XXI(b)(iii), as measures 'taken in time of war or other emergency in international relations' (unlike measures covered by the exceptions under Article XX) does not necessitate a prior determination that they would be WTO-inconsistent if they had been taken in normal times, i.e. if they were not taken in time of war or other emergency in international relations. This is because, for the reasons explained in Section 7.5.6 [of the report], there is no need to determine the extent of the deviation of the challenged measure from the prescribed norm in order to evaluate the necessity of the measure, i.e. that there is no reasonably available alternative measure to achieve the protection of the legitimate interests covered by the exception which is not violative, or is less violative, of the prescribed norm" (para 7.108).

By contrast, it is submitted that the panel should have examined the wording, context, object and purpose of Article XXI(b)(iii), before possibly considering whether it has to be understood as dealing with the abstract concept of a fundamental change of circumstance. Furthermore, the claim view that there is no need to inquire into whether there are reasonably alternative measures (i.e. no need for a necessity analysis at all), is questionable, too, as will be explained below in Sects. 3.4.4.2 and 4.2.3.

[18] Panel report, *Saudi Arabia – IPRs*, para 7.241.

[19] See below, Sect. 3.5.

[20] Cf. the WTO website at https://www.wto.org/english/tratop_e/dispu_e/cases_e/ds567_e.htm (last accessed on 7 December 2022).

non-adopted panel reports[21]—may indeed remain influential, not least since it is the first WTO panel report addressing the security exception in the TRIPS Agreement, which, moreover, confirms the interpretation of the analogous GATT security exception in *Russia – Transit* to a considerable extent.

3.3 Wording and Structure of the Security Exceptions

Article XXI of the GATT is worded as follows:

> **Article XXI: Security Exceptions**
> Nothing in this Agreement shall be construed
>
> (a) to require any contracting party to furnish any information the disclosure of which it considers contrary to its essential security interests; or
> (b) to prevent any contracting party from taking any action which it considers necessary for the protection of its essential security interests
> (i) relating to fissionable materials or the materials from which they are derived;
> (ii) relating to the traffic in arms, ammunition and implements of war and to such traffic in other goods and materials as is carried on directly or indirectly for the purpose of supplying a military establishment;
> (iii) taken in time of war or other emergency in international relations; or
> (c) to prevent any contracting party from taking any action in pursuance of its obligations under the United Nations Charter for the maintenance of international peace and security.

Article XXI(a) and Article XXI(c) of the GATT raise issues that are different from that of Article XXI(b) of the GATT and will not be addressed in this contribution.[22] Instead, the focus will be on Article XXI(b) and the virtually identically worded Article 73(b)(iii) of the TRIPS Agreement.

---

[21] This is also pointed out by Zhou (2020); see also Arato et al. (2020), pp. 627 ff.

[22] Article XXI(c) connects the GATT system with Article 103 of the UN Charter and confirms that obligations under the Charter have priority vis-à-vis GATT obligations. It has been understood as not incurring questions of justification such as those relevant under Article XXI(b) (cf. Van den Bossche and Akpofure (2020); see also Hahn (1996), pp. 288 ff for an analysis of this clause). It is noteworthy, however, that the US has reportedly been including new wording in newly negotiated trade agreements which enables the parties to assess their obligations under the UN Charter themselves (cf. Heath 2020, fn 99).

The right granted to WTO Members under Article XXI(a) not to furnish information, which a Member considers contrary to its essential security interests, had been invoked by Russia in the *Russia – Transit* case (cf. panel report, *Russia – Transit*, paras 7.115 and 7.129), but has not been addressed by the panel. Likewise, Saudi Arabia had referred to "reports by intelligence chiefs. . .the details of which will not be presented in the context of this WTO dispute" (panel report, *Saudi*

In particular, we will have to concentrate on the identical introductory clauses of GATT Article XXI(b) and TRIPS Article 73(b)(iii), according to which "nothing in this Agreement shall be construed. . .to prevent any contracting party from taking any action which it considers necessary for the protection of its essential security interests". These introductory phrases are usually referred to as the "Chapeau" of GATT Article XXI(b) and the "Chapeau" of TRIPS Article 73(b), respectively. Furthermore, we will have to focus on the identical third subparagraphs of GATT Article XXI(b) and TRIPS Article 73(b), in particular on the wording "taken in time of. . .other emergency in international relations". This wording and the respective Chapeaus have given rise to the disputes discussed here as well as most of the debates preceding and following these cases.

3.4 The 2019 *Russia – Transit* Case

3.4.1 Factual Aspects

In February 2019, Ukraine requested the establishment of a WTO dispute settlement panel, claiming that Russia had violated its obligations under the GATT by having imposed transit restrictions inconsistent with the GATT (*in casu* Articles V and X). In response, Russia asserted that it considered these measures necessary "for the protection of its essential security interests" and argued that it had taken them in response to "the emergency in international relations that occurred in 2014", which presented threats to its "essential security interests". Russia therefore invoked Article XXI(b)(iii) of the GATT, claiming that the panel lacked jurisdiction to hear this case.[23]

As explained by the panel, this dispute has to be understood against the background of the 2014 change in government in Ukraine, the ensuing "Euromaidan events" and the signature, by Ukraine, of the EU-Ukraine Association Agreement in 2014. Both Russia and Ukraine did not refer directly to these events. This litigation strategy—in particular the fact that Russia largely refrained from submitting relevant evidence—constituted a challenge for the panel as regards the determination of the relevant factual aspects, which involved the question as to whether there existed a situation amounting to an "emergency in international relations" in the sense of Article XXI(b)(iii) of the GATT. The panel took a first step towards resolving these issues by referring to a 2016 Resolution of the UN General Assembly which condemned the "temporary occupation of parts of the territory of Ukraine" and

Arabia – IPRs, para 2.25). These statements by Russia and Saudi Arabia were not, however, further addressed by the panels. It has been submitted that the application of Article XXI(a) should be seen to be subject, like Article XXI(b), to the requirement of good faith (cf. Hahn (1991), p. 583; see also Van den Bossche and Akpofure (2020) text at fn 173).

[23] Panel report, *Russia – Transit*, paras 7.1–7.4 (quotation at para 7.4).

their "annexation". The panel also emphasized that this Resolution explicitly referred to the 1949 Geneva Conventions, which apply in cases of declared war and armed conflict,[24] and again referred to this Resolution in those parts of its report dealing with the legal assessment of Russia's conduct.[25]

3.4.2 *Pandora's Box: Jurisdiction and Substantive Assessment Intermingled in the Panel Report*

In this case, Russia argued that a WTO Member invoking Article XXI(b)(iii) disposes of the "sole discretion" not only to determine its "essential security interests" in the sense of this provision, but also to decide which measures are necessary to protect these interests, whether to disclose information relevant for its essential security interests, and also to determine what constitutes an "emergency in international relations" within the meaning of subparagraph (iii) as well as whether such emergency exists in a given case.[26]

This line of argument brings us to the core of the problem, as it risks opening the "box of Pandora" of WTO law: if one in fact were to take the view that a WTO Member is free to determine the goal pursued, the means employed and the nexus between means and goals under this provision,[27] then Article XXI(b)(iii) would indeed amount to a "catch-all provision"[28] not subject to judicial review, which would risk incurring the "collapse" of the GATT.[29]

Hence, not least for reasons of *effet utile*, Article XXI(b) can hardly be read as an unlimited "escape clause".[30] As has been submitted in academic writings preceding *Russia – Transit, Saudi Arabia – IPRs* and *US – Steel*, it is obvious that Article XXI (b) should be understood as being subject to limitations, which can quite clearly be inferred from its wording and structure as well as the object and purpose of the GATT and WTO law more generally:[31] one evident restraint has been pointed out in an early study by *Hahn*, who has argued that the three distinct factual situations

[24] Panel report, *Russia – Transit*, paras 7.5–7.8 (the quotation, cited above, in para 7.8 of the panel report refers to UN General Assembly Resolution No. 71/205 of 19 December 2016, A/RES/71/205).

[25] See below, Sect. 3.4.3.

[26] Panel report, *Russia – Transit*, paras 7.27–7.28.

[27] As will be shown below, the structure of Article XXI(b)(iii) can be read in terms of the "*logic of ends and means*" (with a state's "essential security interests" being the end/goal, the "actions" employed being the means, and the "necessity" or "suitability" of the means employed constituting the nexus between ends and means).

[28] Schloemann and Ohlhoff (1999), pp. 441 ff.

[29] Hahn (1991), pp. 586 ff; Schloemann and Ohlhoff (1999), pp. 441 ff.

[30] See in particular Hahn (1991), pp. 585 ff.

[31] On this and relevant considerations in the *Russia – Transit* panel report and academic writings see the following text and footnotes.

enumerated in subparagraphs (i), (ii) and (iii) constitute preconditions that must be fulfilled before a WTO Member can invoke the Chapeau of Article XXI(b)[32] (under which panels may possibly be required to accord more discretion to WTO Members than under the subparagraphs; on this see in the following). In a similar vein, it has been opined in the literature that not all elements of Article XXI(b) are necessarily "self-judging", this question having to be answered for each criterion in Article XXI (b) separately.[33] Furthermore, the negotiating history of Article XXI(b) has been understood as implying that a purely "self-judging" character of this provision had never been intended.[34] Finally, on a more general level, it has been submitted that reading clauses like Article XXI(b) as a jurisdictional exemption would run counter to the inherent competence of panels to decide on their jurisdiction and the principles of *nemo iudex in causa sua* and *pacta sunt servanda*.[35]

The ruling in *Russia – Transit* seems to be clearly inspired by this academic groundwork, as it partly resembles an assemblage of these considerations, fit, by the panel, into the order of interpretative steps suggested by Articles 31–33 of the VCLT. Having recalled Appellate Body jurisprudence according to which WTO panels possess inherent jurisdiction to determine their own substantive jurisdiction, the panel inferred from Articles 1.1 and 7 and Appendix 2 of the DSU[36] that it is competent to assess Russia's invocation of Article XXI(b)(iii) of the GATT, since these DSU provisions do not set forth special rules for disputes in which Article XXI of the GATT is invoked.[37] As has rightly been observed, the panel should have affirmed and stopped the examination of its jurisdiction on the basis of this reasoning[38] (as has in fact been done by the panel in *Saudi Arabia*, as will be seen below).

However, since Russia had claimed that Article XXI(b)(iii) is "self-judging", the panel went on to examine whether this provision "carves out from a panel's jurisdiction *ratione materiae* actions" considered necessary by a WTO Member for the protection of its essential security interests in the sense of Article XXI(b) (iii). In the ensuing reasoning, the panel undertook a full-fledged interpretation of this provision,[39] which is preponderantly relevant for the substantive assessment of Russia's conduct, but is presented in the panel report as relating to questions of both jurisdiction and justiciability. As mentioned above, this approach, which is confusing and has been criticized by some WTO Members,[40] may be due to the fact that the

---

[32] Hahn (1991), pp. 585 ff; see also Schloemann and Ohlhoff (1999), pp. 441 ff.

[33] Hahn (1991), pp. 585 ff; Schloemann and Ohlhoff (1999), pp. 430 ff; Akande and Williams (2003), pp. 381 ff; see also Schill and Briese (2009), pp. 106 ff (submitting that most writer agree on this issue).

[34] Bogdanova (2021), p. 132; Hahn (1991), pp. 562–563.

[35] Schill and Briese (2009), pp. 119–120.

[36] This line of argument had also been pointed out by Akande and Williams (2003), pp. 378 ff.

[37] Panel report, *Russia – Transit*, paras 7.53–7.56.

[38] Van den Bossche and Akpofure (2020), text at fn 41.

[39] Van den Bossche and Akpofure (2020), text at fn 42.

[40] Van den Bossche and Akpofure (2020), fn 48.

issues of jurisdiction, justiciability, substantive assessment and deference are not always clearly distinguished in the literature discussing the concept of (allegedly) "self-judging" provisions.

Thus, the panel turned to the interpretation of Article XXI(b), first addressing the issue as to whether the key clause "which it considers" in the Chapeau—which is often read as implying a "self-judging" character of Article XXI(b)—(i) merely qualifies the term "necessary", (ii) whether it qualifies both the term "necessary" and the determination of the "essential security interests" invoked by a WTO Member, or (iii) whether it also extends to the three subparagraphs of Article XXI(b), qualifying the latter as well. Like the aforementioned writings, the panel inferred from the structure of Article XXI(b) and considerations of *effet utile* that the subparagraphs function as "limitative qualifying clauses" that restrict "the exercise of the discretion accorded to [WTO] Members under the chapeau" to the circumstances defined in the subparagraphs.[41]

In the next step, the panel inquired into whether the criteria laid down in the three subparagraphs of Article XXI(b) have to be regarded as lending themselves to a "purely subjective discretionary determination".[42] It had already been argued in the literature, in particular by *Hahn*, that subparagraphs (i) and (ii) lay down *objective* preconditions; moreover, it had also been submitted that the term "war" in subparagraph (iii) is a term of international law, not domestic law.[43] Hence, if one regarded the term "emergency in international relations" as allowing a purely subjective—and thus potentially overly broad—determination, one would run the risk that the other objective preconditions in the subparagraphs could easily be circumvented. Adopting a similar systematic-teleological approach of interpretation, the panel argued that the terms "relating to" in subparagraphs (i) and (ii)—like their counterpart "relating to" in Article XX(g) of the GATT—constitute objective requirements. Against this background, the panel concluded that the term "taken in time of war" in subparagraph (iii) should be understood as constituting "an objective fact, amenable to objective determination".[44] Extending this systematic-teleological line of argument, the panel concluded that the cardinal term "emergency in international relations" requires objective determination, too.[45]

The panel then imposed further restrictions on the concept "emergency in international relations". It inferred these from this notion's ordinary meaning and immediate context in Article XXI(b), which according to the panel imply that this term encompasses "defence and military interests, as well as maintenance of law and public order interests".[46] Furthermore, as had similarly been submitted in the

[41] Panel report, *Russia – Transit*, paras 7.62–7.65 (quotations at para 7.65).

[42] Panel report, *Russia – Transit*, paras 7.62 ff (quotation at para 7.66).

[43] Cf. in particular Hahn (1991), pp. 586 ff.

[44] Panel report, *Russia – Transit*, para 7.69–7.70 (quotation at para 7.70).

[45] Panel report, *Russia – Transit*, para 7.71.

[46] Panel report, *Russia – Transit*, para 7.74.

literature,[47] the panel stressed that "political or economic differences between Members are not sufficient, of themselves, to constitute an emergency in international relations" in the sense of this provision, "unless they give rise to defence and military interests, or maintenance of law and public order interests".[48] Moreover, the panel held that an emergency in international relations refers "generally to a situation of armed conflict, or of latent armed conflict, or of heightened tension or crisis, or general instability engulfing or surrounding a state".[49]

The panel found its interpretation confirmed by the object and purpose of the GATT and the WTO Agreement more generally, as both are meant to promote legal security and predictability in international trade relations. As underlined by the panel, interpreting Article XXI as a "self-judging" exception would be "entirely contrary" to this object and purpose.[50] The panel further held that the practice of the Contracting Parties of the GATT 1947 and the Members of the WTO do not amount to a subsequent practice in the application of the GATT which establishes an agreement of the parties regarding the interpretation of Article XXI in the sense of Article 31(3)(b) of the VCLT. It stressed, however, that the "significant majority of occasions", on which Article XXI(b)(iii) had been invoked, endorsed its aforementioned interpretation of this provision.[51] The panel additionally argued that it had found further endorsement of its interpretative result in the *travaux préparatoires* of Article XXI.[52] Although it has been questioned in the literature whether the panel's summary of the negotiating history is fully to the point,[53] the panel had in any case clearly based its reasoning on the wording, context and object and purpose of Article XXI(b)(iii).[54]

The panel therefore concluded that, contrary to what had been submitted by Russia, Article XXI(b)(iii) is neither "totally self-judging" in the sense of ousting a panel's *jurisdiction*, nor self-judging in the sense of being "*non-justiciable*" (as had been claimed by the US as third party in these proceedings).[55] This dual finding, which relates to *both* jurisdiction and justiciability, again underlines that the panel in this part of the report has intermingled questions of jurisdiction, substantive assessment and standard of review.[56]

[47] Hahn (1991), pp. 578 ff.

[48] Panel report, *Russia – Transit*, para 7.75.

[49] Panel report, *Russia – Transit*, para 7.76 (italics added).

[50] Panel report, *Russia – Transit*, para 7.79.

[51] Panel report, *Russia – Transit*, para 7.80 and the Appendix of this report.

[52] Panel report, *Russia – Transit*, para 7.83–7.100.

[53] Van den Bossche and Akpofure (2020), text following fn 115.

[54] Van den Bossche and Akpofure (2020), text following fn 115.

[55] Panel report, *Russia – Transit*, paras 7.102–7.103 (quotation at para 7.102; italics added).

[56] See also Van den Bossche and Akpofure (2020), text at fn 41.

3.4.3 Interpretation and further Substantive Assessment

After this interim conclusion, the panel, in its rather meandering approach, returned to the interpretation and application of the terms "taken in time of. . .emergency in international relations". In this section of the report, the panel above all appears concerned with the burden of proof laid on, and the degree of deference to be accorded to, the respondent under Article XXI(b)(iii). It is critical in this regard that Russia, as indicated above, had adopted a rather obscure approach in discharging its burden of proof, in that it merely referred to "an emergency in international relations that occurred in 2014" that was "well known to Ukraine", which had led it to impose the measures at issue.[57] Furthermore, rather than characterizing the actual situation, Russia referred to hypothetical situations "in order not to introduce. . .some information that [it] cannot disclose". In this context, Russia also referred to a 2016 report of the WTO Trade Policy Review Mechanism (TPRM), which mentions the "annexation" of Crimea and "the military conflict in the east".[58]

Despite these indirect references and although in prior disputes WTO panels had declined to make use of TPRM reports, the panel found that Russia had sufficiently identified the situation which Russia considered to be an "emergency in international relations" in terms of Article XXI(b)(iii).[59] The panel then complemented the analysis by referring to the aforementioned 2016 Resolution of the UN General Assembly and the fact that several states had imposed sanctions against Russia in connection with this situation.[60] On the basis of this evidence, added by the panel itself to Russia's rather allusive indications, the panel concluded that the situation at issue indeed constituted an emergency in international relations in terms of Article XXI(b)(iii).[61]

This finding is remarkable for several reasons. On the one hand, it has been noted that many WTO Members in the past had taken the view that panels must not second-guess a WTO Member's determination as to whether an emergency in international relations actually exists,[62] a view which had also been advanced in academic writings.[63] The panel in this case, however, clearly inquired into whether such an emergency was present. Yet, as has been submitted by commentators, the threshold set by the panel for the burden of proof in *Russia – Transit* appears quite, if not unduly, low.[64]

---

[57] Panel report, *Russia – Transit*, para 7.112.

[58] Panel report, *Russia – Transit*, para 7.115; on this see also Glöckle (2019), pp. 656–657.

[59] Panel report, *Russia – Transit*, para 7.119.

[60] Panel report, *Russia – Transit*, para 7.122.

[61] Panel report, *Russia – Transit*, para 7.123.

[62] Vidigal (2019), pp. 210–211.

[63] Cf. Akande and Williams (2003), pp. 381 ff.

[64] Cf. Van den Bossche and Akpofure (2020), text at fn 134–135, arguing that the burden of proof should be stepped up in future cases.

Furthermore, in view of the panel's considerations relating to the interpretation of the concept "emergency in international relations",[65] the report has been read as implying that the panel required a nexus with the traditional concept of militarized security[66] (thus apparently rejecting the aforementioned current trends in which the concept of security tends to be expanded considerably beyond the military context[67]). In contrast, the panel's aforementioned nuanced reasoning that "political or economic differences between Members are not sufficient, *of themselves*, to constitute an emergency in international relations", "unless they give rise to defence and military interests, *or* maintenance of law and public order interests",[68] could possibly also be read as leaving the door open for an invocation of Article XXI(b)(iii) in cases of serious economic crises that incur grave public order interests.[69]

Moreover, in view of the qualification by the panel that an emergency in international relations refers "generally to a situation of armed conflict, or of latent armed conflict, or of heightened tension or crisis, or general instability *engulfing or surrounding* a state", it has been submitted that countries like the US could not rely on Article XXI in order to justify e.g. sanctions imposed for reasons of human rights violation in distant countries.[70] On the other hand, it has been argued that the 2022 Russian invasion of the Ukraine could be seen as a threat to the national security of the US.[71] Similarly, it has been submitted e.g. that Canada could invoke Article XXI regarding the sanctions it adopted—like many other countries[72]—against Russia in 2022, in view of the fact that according to the panel's ruling a WTO Member need not be directly involved in an armed conflict.[73]

Moving on to the remaining element of subparagraph (iii) of Article XXI(b), the question as to whether the actions at issue were "taken in time of" this emergency in international relations, the panel noted that Russia had imposed its measures "during" the emergency. It concluded that this requirement was fulfilled, therefore.[74] In light of the rather restrictive concept "during", doubts have been voiced as to

[65] Cf. above, Sect. 3.4.2.

[66] Cohen (2020), p. 806.

[67] Cf. above, Chap. 2.

[68] Panel report, *Russia – Transit*, para 7.75 (italics added).

[69] See also Glöckle (2019), pp. 626 ff (emphasizing that the panel seems to have decoupled the security exception from a narrow military context); and Van den Bossche and Akpofure (2020), text at fn 126 ff, making a similar point. Contra e.g. Weiß (2020), pp. 831 ff. The 2022 panel reports in *US – Steel* seem to have excluded the possibility of invoking the security exception in most cases of economic emergencies (see below, Sect. 3.6.3).

[70] Cf. Bogdanova (2021), pp. 193 ff, who also discusses this practice of the US and other states.

[71] Paulsen (2022).

[72] Cf. e.g. Collins (2022).

[73] Ranjan (2022); this corresponds to the view taken by the US during the negotiations of Article XXI, in which the US delegate explained that Article XXI had been drafted with the situation of the US in mind before the US entered World War II (cf. the panel report, *Russia – Transit*, fn 152).

[74] Panel report, *Russia – Transit*, para 7.124.

whether measures such as those taken by the US in the Huawei context[75] or trade restrictions and economic sanctions taken e.g. to prevent and punish cyber-attacks could be justified under Article XXI.[76]

3.4.4 Analysis of the Chapeau

Moving on to the interpretation of the Chapeau of Article XXI(b), the panel in *Russia – Transit* returned to the aforementioned question as to whether the central wording "which it considers" in the Chapeau (i) merely qualifies the term "necessary", (ii) whether it qualifies both the term "necessary" and the determination of the "essential security interests" invoked, or (iii) whether it also extends to the three subparagraphs of Article XXI(b), qualifying the latter as well. In its considerations under subparagraph (iii), the panel had clearly ruled out the third possibility, as it had found that subparagraph (iii)—like subparagraphs (i) and (ii)—constitutes an objective limitative clause.[77]

Under the Chapeau, the panel therefore continued with an inquiry into the remaining two alternatives. Whereas the panel, as indicated, had intermingled questions of jurisdiction, substantive assessment and deference in its considerations relating to subparagraph (iii),[78] its reasoning under the Chapeau is clearly concerned with the issues of interpretation and deference.

3.4.4.1 Essential Security Interests and Good Faith Review

In prior academic writings it had been submitted that the principle of good faith—which is commonly regarded as general principle of law and a principle of general international law[79]—should be considered relevant also in the interpretation of the Chapeau.[80] In light of this principle and contextual arguments (namely that due to Article XXI(a) of the GATT a WTO Member is not required to disclose information which it considers contrary to its essential security interests), it had been posited that WTO panels are not competent to decide whether an "essential security interest" exists and whether it is actually threatened; accordingly, a panel only ought to

---

[75] The term "Huawei-style sanctions" has been used in the literature to refer to import and export restrictions imposed by the US against Chinese companies like, in particular, Huawei and its affiliates for security reasons (cf. Bogdanova (2021), pp. 188 ff).

[76] Bogdanova (2021), pp. 193 ff.

[77] Cf. above, Sect. 3.4.2.

[78] Cf. above, Sect. 3.4.2.

[79] Cf. e.g. Kolb (2017), pp. 3 ff et passim.

[80] Cf. e.g. Hahn (1991), pp. 597 ff; Schill and Briese (2009), pp. 120 ff; Akande and Williams (2003), pp. 381 ff.

determine whether the WTO Member *itself* "considered its essential security interests to be threatened and considered the measure taken to be proportionate to addressing that threat"[81] (a view also taken by the US in *US – Steel*, as will be seen in the following). However, it has also been maintained that the principle of good faith implies that Article XXI(b) must not be abused,[82] which has in particular been understood to mean that Article XXI(b) must not be relied upon in order to justify protectionist measures.[83] Furthermore, regarding the question as to how the review of good faith should be operationalized,[84] it has e.g. been argued that the principles of reasonableness and proportionality should be regarded as limits to a WTO Member's discretion.[85] Moreover, it has been claimed that the good faith test could be operationalized through a procedural review.[86] Both approaches have also been applied by the Appellate Body in past rulings.[87]

The panel in *Russia – Transit* clearly held itself called upon to determine, albeit it with considerable deference, whether a WTO Member's essential security interests are at stake. It first indicated that the term "essential" has a narrowing quality and hence defined "essential security interests" as having to "*generally* be understood [as referring to] interests relating to the quintessential functions of the state, namely, the protection of its territory and its population from external threats, and the maintenance of law and public order internally".[88] Since these interests may vary depending on changing circumstances, the panel reasoned that "it is left, *in general*, to every Member to define what it considers to be its essential security interests".[89]

While these formulas appear broad, it should be emphasized, first, that they comprise limitations themselves (in the form of the wording "generally" and "it is left, in general"). Secondly, the discretion *prima facie* accorded to the respondent WTO Member will only be brought to bear in cases where the preconditions set forth in subparagraph (iii), as interpreted by the panel,[90] are fulfilled. Thirdly, the panel

---

[81] Akande and Williams (2003), pp. 381 ff (quotation at 399).

[82] Hahn (1991), pp. 597 ff.

[83] Schill and Briese (2009), pp. 106 ff.

[84] On this cf. in particular Schill and Briese (2009), pp. 120 ff.

[85] Schloemann and Ohlhoff (1999), pp. 444–445; Schill and Briese (2009), pp. 106 ff; Akande and Williams (2003), p. 399; see also Van den Bossche and Akpofure (2020), text at fn 154 ff.

[86] Schill and Briese (2009), pp. 136 ff.

[87] Cf. Van den Bossche and Akpofure (2020), text at fn 154 ff, pointing out that the good faith review had involved objective elements such as proportionality and reasonableness in the reports of the Appellate Body in *US – Shrimp* on the one hand and a procedural scrutiny in the *US – FSC* case (cf. Appellate Body Report, *United States – Import Prohibition of Certain Shrimp and Shrimp Products*, WT/DS58/AB/R, adopted 6 November 1998, DSR 1998:VII, 2755; Appellate Body Report, *United States – Tax Treatment for "Foreign Sales Corporations"*, WT/DS108/AB/R, adopted 20 March 2000, DSR 2000:III, 1619). On the issue of the operationalization of the good faith review under Article XXI(b) see below, Chap. 4.

[88] Panel report, *Russia – Transit*, para 7.130 (italics added).

[89] Panel report, *Russia – Transit*, para 7.131 (italics added).

[90] Cf. above, Sects. 3.4.2 and 3.4.3.

articulated further restraints, which it derived—similarly to the aforementioned academic writings—from the principle of good faith. Accordingly, the panel held that Article XXI cannot be invoked in order to circumvent obligations under the GATT, by e.g. "simply re-labelling trade interests that it had agreed to protect and promote within the system, as 'essential security interests', falling outside the reach of that system".[91]

In this context, the panel expressly circumscribed the burden of argumentation, which is incumbent on a respondent relying on Article XXI, by requiring the latter "to articulate the essential security interests...sufficiently enough to demonstrate their *veracity*".[92] The panel held in a finding which deserves to be quoted in full:

> What qualifies as a sufficient level of articulation will depend on the emergency in international relations at issue. In particular, the Panel considers that *the less characteristic* is the 'emergency in international relations' invoked by the Member, i.e. *the further it is removed from* armed conflict, or a situation of breakdown of law and public order (whether in the invoking Member or in its immediate surroundings), the less obvious are the defence or military interests, or maintenance of law and public order interests, that can be generally expected to arise. In such cases, a Member would need to articulate its essential security interests *with greater specificity* than would be required when the emergency in international relations involved, for example, armed conflict.[93]

Hence, the panel has evidently taken a procedural approach to the determination of the "essential security interests" standard as well as to the interrelated concretization of the principle of good faith, by imposing a duty to give reasons on the respondent. In this context, the decisive consideration can be expressed through the formula "the further removed from armed conflict – the greater the need to articulate essential security interests with sufficient specificity". In other words: the closer an emergency in international relations is to armed conflict, the more plausible it appears *prima facie* that a WTO Member's essential security interests may be at stake and the lower the burden of argumentation will accordingly be.

In academic comments, it has been suggested in this context that the panel's "less stringent approach of good faith judicial review" seems insufficient "to draw a clear line between protection and protectionism".[94] While it is true that drawing a line between protective and protectionist measures is notoriously difficult, this critique arguably overlooks the "sliding scale" approach[95] that the panel has introduced in order to adjust the burden of argumentation in correspondence with the degree of plausibility that appears suitable depending on the circumstances of the concrete case at issue. It arguably seems difficult to achieve more as a starting point in rational argumentation that is concerned with balancing competing interests.

---

[91] Panel report, *Russia – Transit*, para 7.133.

[92] Panel report, *Russia – Transit*, para 7.134.

[93] Panel report, *Russia – Transit*, para 7.135 (italics added). On the divergent approach of the panel in *Saudi Arabia – IPRs* see below, Sect. 3.5.

[94] Roberts et al. (2019), p. 665 and fn 54.

[95] Van den Bossche and Akpofure (2020), fn 162 with further references.

Having set out this nuanced standard for the burden of argumentation, the panel had to address yet another particularity of this case, namely that Russia, in line with its litigation strategy,[96] had not explicitly articulated its "essential security interests" in the sense of the Chapeau either. However, in view of the fact that Russia had referred to "certain characteristics of the 2014 emergency" and the fact that this emergency had been recognized by the UN General Assembly as an armed conflict,[97] the panel concluded that "[d]espite its allusiveness, Russia's articulation of its essential security interests is minimally satisfactory". Hence, the burden of argumentation for the respondent under the Chapeau was set equally low as under subparagraph (iii)[98] in this case. However, this arguably is in line with the panel's "sliding scale" approach, given that the case at issue had clearly been recognized as involving armed conflict by the UN and on the international level more generally. Moreover, applying the concept of food faith, the panel found that there were no indications that Russia had invoked Article XXI(b)(iii) so as to merely circumvent its GATT obligations.[99]

3.4.4.2 The Nexus Between Ends and Means: Mere Plausibility?

The panel then addressed the connection between the essential security interests at stake and the measures taken by Russia, emphasizing that in its view the principle of good faith also qualifies this relationship between ends and means. In this respect, the panel held that the measures adopted need to "meet a minimum requirement of plausibility in relation to the proffered essential security interests", which means, according to the panel, that the actions adopted must not be "implausible as measures protective of these interests".[100] In the concrete case, the panel found that the Russian measures met this—very low—"not implausible" standard.

While this modest threshold set by the panel for analysing the suitability of the measure at issue can be explained in terms of legal methodology,[101] the remainder of the panel's reasoning appears problematic. Thus, the panel strikingly and quite tersely held that, since the plausibility hurdle had been cleared by Russia, "it is *for Russia to determine* the 'necessity' of the measures for the protection of its essential security interests".[102] Pursuant to the panel, this "conclusion follows by logical necessity if the adjectival clause 'which it considers' is to be given legal effect".[103]

---

[96] See above, Sect. 3.4.1.

[97] See above, Sect. 3.4.1.

[98] On this cf. above, Sects. 3.4.2 and 3.4.3.

[99] Panel report, *Russia – Transit*, para 7.137.

[100] Panel report, *Russia – Transit*, para 7.138.

[101] See below, Sect. 4.2.2.2.

[102] Panel report, *Russia – Transit*, para 7.146 (italics added).

[103] By way of explanation, the panel here (in para 7.146) referred to the "negotiating history" of Article XXI as presented in para 7.92 of its report. However, para 7.92 merely restates a declaration

This finding appears surprising and questionable. On the one hand, it does not correspond to the wording of Article XXI(b), which employs the term "necessary". On the other hand, it is not in line with long-standing jurisprudence on the "general exceptions" clause of Article XX of the GATT, where the term "necessary" is central in several paragraphs.[104] Furthermore, omitting the issue of necessity altogether in the context of systematic-teleological interpretation in a rule vs exception constellation (and likewise in the analysis of the interplay between ends and means) is questionable for reasons of legal methodology, as will be shown below.[105] Similarly, not addressing the question of necessity under the concept of good faith (or related concepts such as the prohibitions on abuse of rights and circumvention, reasonableness and proportionality) appears problematic, given that the tests of proportionality and its subtests of suitability and necessity can be understood as concretizations of the principle of good faith.[106]

In addition, it is difficult to see that the panel's conclusion follows by "logical necessity", as claimed by the panel, from the clause "which it considers" in Article XXI(b): the latter qualification could, and arguably should, be understood as a requirement for panels to exercise deference *within* the necessity analysis.[107] Finally, the reasoning of the panel is debatable in that it defined the necessity test as requiring scrutiny as to whether "there is no reasonably available alternative measure to achieve the protection of the legitimate interests covered by the exception which is not violative, or is *less violative*, of the prescribed norm".[108] However, in terms of legal methodology, a *norm* can either be violated or not; there is no question of degrees. It is arguably for this reason, too, that WTO jurisprudence addressing the concept of necessity under Article XX of the GATT has deviated from the test of whether a hypothetical alternative measure "is not violative, or is less violative" of GATT *norms* and has for several years now inquired in particular into whether there is an alternative measure which is less restrictive of *trade*.[109] Thirdly, there is an extensive jurisprudence by the Appellate Body as to the degree of deference that is called for under the necessity test under Article XX of the GATT,[110] which arguably should be examined as to its relevance for Article XXI of the GATT as well.

---

of the US delegate in discussions during the drafting of Article XXI, which, moreover, does not address the issue of necessity.

[104] For an overview of relevant rulings see Van den Bossche and Zdouc (2022), pp. 592 ff.

[105] See below, Sects. 4.2.2 and 4.2.3.

[106] See also below, Sect. 4.2.

[107] This is also the view expressed e.g. by the EU in the *US – Steel* dispute (European Union, Opening Oral Statement, *United States – Certain Measures on Steel and Aluminium Products*, DS548, Geneva, 4 November 2019, paras 90, 122).

[108] Panel report, *Russia – Transit*, para 108.

[109] Cf. e.g. Van den Bossche and Zdouc (2022), pp. 608, 637 and fn 73; see also Vranes (2009), pp. 269 ff with further references.

[110] Cf. e.g. Van den Bossche and Zdouc (2022), pp. 592 ff and 656 ff; Vranes (2009), pp. 271 ff.

3.5 The 2020 *Saudi Arabia – IPRs* Case

3.5.1 Factual Aspects

In November 2019, Qatar brought a complaint against Saudi Arabia, arguing that Saudi Arabia had infringed its obligations under the TRIPS Agreement (i) by having adopted a set of measures that resulted in preventing the Qatar-based media group BeIN from obtaining legal counsel to enforce its TRIPS rights through civil enforcement procedures in Saudi Arabia and (ii) by having omitted to apply criminal procedures and penalties to the Saudi company beoutQ which was alleged to have exploited the rights held by BeIN.[111]

The panel emphasized that this dispute has to be understood in the light of the "serious deterioration of relations" between the WTO Members involved in this dispute, which had led Saudi Arabia to sever all relations with Qatar in 2017.[112] Saudi Arabia in particular claimed that Qatar supported terrorists and extremists, allowed "them to use Qatar-based and Qatar-sponsored media platforms to spread their messages" and was engaged in activities threatening the security and stability of the Gulf Cooperation Council countries. In the latter regard, Saudi Arabia referred to intelligence reports, the details of which it declared would not be presented in the context of the WTO dispute.[113]

3.5.2 Jurisdiction

As indicated above, unlike Russia in the *Russia – Transit* dispute, Saudi Arabia had not explicitly referred to the concepts of "jurisdiction" or "justiciability".[114] However, its arguments that the dispute with Qatar was "no trade dispute at all", but a "political, geopolitical and essential security dispute",[115] were construed by several third parties as implying that Saudi Arabia regarded the case as "non-justiciable".[116] Like the panel in *Russia – Transit*, the *Saudi Arabia – IPRs* panel found that it had jurisdiction to hear this case, although it relied on a different reasoning, due to the manner in which Saudi Arabia had presented its case. Thus, Saudi Arabia's arguments were understood by the panel as raising the question as to whether it disposes of the discretion to decline to *exercise* jurisdiction, which had in principle been established in conformity with the DSU.[117] Since Qatar's complaint was restricted to

[111] Panel report, *Saudi Arabia – IPRs*, paras 7.1 ff.

[112] Panel report, *Saudi Arabia – IPRs*, paras 2.16 ff.

[113] Panel report, *Saudi Arabia – IPRs*, para 2.25.

[114] Cf. above, Sect. 3.1.

[115] Panel report, *Saudi Arabia – IPRs*, para 7.8.

[116] Panel report, *Saudi Arabia – IPRs*, para 7.9.

[117] Panel report, *Saudi Arabia – IPRs*, paras 7.7–7.10 (quotations at para 7.9).

the TRIPS Agreement and did not concern the broader dispute between Saudi Arabia and Qatar, the panel found that it was bound to exercise its jurisdiction and that the matter in dispute was justiciable as well.[118]

3.5.3 Interpretation and Substantive Assessment

3.5.3.1 The Legal Standard as Defined by the Panel

As regards the order of analysis, the panel in *Saudi Arabia – IPRs*, in contrast to the panel in *Russia – Transit*, first examined whether *Saudi Arabia* had violated any of its substantive obligations under WTO law. Only after having found that Saudi Arabia had indeed acted inconsistently with its obligations under the TRIPS Agreement,[119] did it move on to analyse whether these infringements could be justified under the relevant security exception, in this case Article 73(b)(iii) of the TRIPS Agreement. Hence, in contradistinction to the panel in *Russia – Transit*, but in line with the common understanding, the *Saudi Arabia – Transit* panel treated the security exception as an affirmative defence.

The panel then spelled out the applicable legal standard, opining that it must assess

(a) "whether the existence of 'a war or other emergency in international relations' has been established in the sense of subparagraph (iii) to Article 73(b);
(b) whether the relevant actions were 'taken in time of' that war or other emergency in international relations;
(c) whether the invoking Member has articulated its relevant 'essential security interests' sufficiently to enable an assessment of whether there is any *link* between those actions and the protection of its essential security interests; and
(d) whether the relevant actions are so remote from, or unrelated to, the 'emergency in international relations' as to make it *implausible* that the invoking Member considers those actions to be *necessary* for the protection of its essential security interests arising out of the emergency".[120]

Although the panel claimed that the analytical framework defined in the *Russia – Transit* panel report "can guide" its assessment, a closer look reveals that the panel in *Saudi Arabia – IPRs* has in fact deviated from this structure on central points. First, the panel in *Russia – Transit* had required the respondent "to articulate the essential security interests said to arise from the emergency in international relations sufficiently enough to demonstrate their *veracity*". The *Saudi Arabia – IPRs* panel, in contrast, related the requirement of sufficient articulation to the *link* between ends

[118] Panel report, *Saudi Arabia – IPRs*, paras 7.10–7.23.
[119] Namely Articles 42, Article 41.1 and 61 of the TRIPS Agreement.
[120] Panel report, *Saudi Arabia – IPRs*, para 7.242 (italics added).

(the essential security interests at stake) and means (the measures actually employed; cf. point c. in the enumeration above). Secondly, the *Russia – Transit* panel report had found that it must review "whether the measures are so remote from, or unrelated to, the [. . .] emergency that it is implausible that [the respondent had] implemented the measures for the protection of its essential security interests arising out of the emergency"[121] and had held that it must not inquire into the necessity of the measures at issue.[122] In contradistinction, in its aforementioned statement the *Saudi Arabia – IPRs* panel connected the "implausibility" standard to the *necessity* of the measures (point d. above). As will be seen below, the panel indeed at least implicitly appeared to take questions of necessity into account in its assessment of the respondent's measures.

3.5.3.2 Application to the Facts

In its substantive assessment, the panel first addressed the question as to whether an "emergency in international relations" *existed* between the parties in this dispute. In this respect, the panel referred to the fact that Saudi Arabia, as indicated, had severed diplomatic, consular and economic relations with Qatar as well as to the fact that Saudi Arabia had "repeatedly alleged" that Qatar *inter alia* "supported terrorism and extremism [. . .] and interfered in the internal affairs of other countries". The panel concluded on the basis of these facts that a situation of emergency in international relations in terms of Article 73(b)(iii) of the TRIPS Agreement existed.[123] In this context, Japan, as a third party, had argued that the assertion that the severance of economic and diplomatic ties constitutes in itself such an emergency under Article 73 (b)(iii) amounts to "circular reasoning".[124] The panel rejected this view by stressing that the "action" that it must examine under the Chapeau of Article 73(b) is not the severance of diplomatic and economic relations, but the measures violating TRIPS obligations. This argument of the panel seems hardly convincing, given that the panel, in this part of its report, was not concerned with the measures taken by Saudi Arabia but the determination of the existence of an "emergency in international relations".

While divergent views had been advanced in these proceedings as to whether panels should exercise deference in determining whether such emergency exists, the panel avoided this issue by emphasizing its view that the existence of this situation had been sufficiently established on the basis of relevant evidence. Moreover, it found that the Saudi Arabian measures had been taken "in time of" this

[121] Panel report, *Russia – Transit*, para 7.139.

[122] Cf. above, Sect. 3.4.4.

[123] Panel report, *Saudi Arabia – IPRs*, paras 7.256–7.270 (quotation at para 7.263).

[124] Panel report, *Saudi Arabia – IPRs*, para 7.238.

emergency.[125] Hence, the requirements of the third paragraph of Article 73(b) were found to be fulfilled.

The panel therefore turned to an examination of the situation under the Chapeau of Article 73(b). Since Saudi Arabia had expressly submitted that its measures were taken to protect itself "from the dangers of terrorism and extremism", the panel found that Saudi Arabia had sufficiently articulated its "essential security interests" in the sense of the low benchmark set in the *Russia – Transit* case.[126] Moreover, the panel maintained that the assessment of a WTO Member's essential security interests is subject to limited review, as "this analytical step serves primarily to provide a benchmark against which to examine [the defendant's measures] under the Chapeau". Hence, as indicated above,[127] the panel did not apply the "sufficient articulation" standard defined by the *Russia – Transit* panel in order to determine the "veracity" of the essential security interests, but merely to "enable an assessment of whether there is *any link* between the relevant actions and the protection of [the respondent's] essential security interests".[128] This central shift of focus from "veracity" to the relationship between interests pursued and actions employed has not, however, been explained by the panel.

Addressing this connection between ends and means, the panel found that the measures taken by Saudi Arabia in order to prevent the Qatari enterprise beIN from obtaining Saudi legal counsel to enforce its IPR rights in Saudi Arabia were not "implausible as measures protective of" Saudia Arabia's essential security interests.[129] However, the panel found that the second set of measures adopted by Saudi Arabia—namely the non-application of criminal procedures and penalties to the Saudi company BoutQ—was so remote from the concrete emergency in international relations "as to make it implausible" that the measures had been implemented by Saudi Arabia "for the protection of its 'essential security interests'".[130]

It is noticeable in this regard that the panel reasoned that the non-application of criminal procedures and penalties to the Saudi company at issue had affected not only Qatar, "but also a range of third-party right holders".[131] This argument could also be read as an implicit application of a necessity test, given that one can assert that this measure is not necessary, as it is overly restrictive of trade in the sense of the necessity test traditionally applied in the context of provisions such as Article XX of

[125] Panel report, *Saudi Arabia – IPRs*, para 7.269 (the panel held that the "measures at issue are of a continuing nature, as opposed to acts or omissions that occurred or were completed on a particular date, and neither party has suggested that the Panel must assign any dates to them for the purposes of examining the claims and defences before the Panel").

[126] See above, Sect. 3.4.4.1.

[127] Cf. above, Sect. 3.5.3.1.

[128] Panel report, *Saudi Arabia – IPRs*, para 7.282.

[129] Panel report, *Saudi Arabia – IPRs*, para 7.285.

[130] Panel report, *Saudi Arabia – IPRs*, para 7.293.

[131] Panel report, *Saudi Arabia – IPRs*, para 7.291.

the GATT. Hence, in this reading, the *Saudi Arabia – IPRs* panel report deviates from its predecessor in *Russia – Transit* on yet another material issue.

In sum, this case shows that the WTO security exceptions do not amount to a "carte blanche", as a WTO Member may fail to successfully invoke them even under the low standard of review applied by the panels under the Chapeaus of Article XXI (b) of the GATT and Article 73(b) of the TRIPS Agreement.

3.6 The 2022 *US – Steel* Cases

3.6.1 Factual Aspects

In 2018, the US had imposed additional duties and related measures on steel and aluminium products, claiming that it considered these measures necessary for national security reasons. In reaction, nine WTO Members brought complaints against the US. The WTO appointed identical panelists for all disputes, who tried to harmonize the time-schedules of these proceedings, but kept the proceedings separate. Four of these disputes have been settled or terminated; in two proceedings the panel reports have not been issued so far.[132] After delays caused by the COVID-19 pandemic and the complexities of the disputes,[133] the panel reports in four proceedings, triggered by China, Norway, Switzerland and Turkey, were issued in December 2022.

The complaints brought by the latter four WTO Members differed in part as regards the measures and claims at issue.[134] However, all four disputes comprised complaints under the GATT and the WTO Agreement on Safeguards. Since the US had invoked Article XXI of the GATT as a defence in all of these proceedings, the findings in these four panel reports are virtually identical as respects Article XXI (as well as the relationship between the Safeguards Agreement and Article XXI of the GATT). In the following, reference will therefore be made only to the dispute between China and the US.

[132] Thus, in 2022 the EU as one of these nine complainants informed the DSB about its withdrawal of the complaint; the EU and the US moreover notified the DSB that they had agreed to resort to arbitration pursuant to Article 25.2 of the DSU and had "immediately and indefinitely suspended" the arbitration (cf. https://www.wto.org/english/tratop_e/dispu_e/cases_e/ds548_e.htm, last accessed on 12 December 2022). The proceedings started by Canada and Mexico have also been settled through mutually agreed solutions. In the proceedings started by India and Russia, the panel informed the DSB that due to the complexity of the dispute, the panel expected to issue its final report to the parties no earlier than the last quarter of 2022 (cf. https://www.wto.org/english/tratop_e/dispu_e/dispu_status_e.htm, last accessed on 12 December 2022).

[133] Cf. the WTO website at https://www.wto.org/english/tratop_e/dispu_e/cases_e/ds544_e.htm, accessed 5 January 2023.

[134] Panel report, *US – Steel (China)*, para 1.21.

3.6.2 *Order of Analysis and Relationship Between the GATT and the Safeguards Agreement*

Regarding the order of analysis, the panel deviated from the report in *Russia – Transit*, in that it followed the traditional approach of first determining whether the US as the respondent had violated any of the substantive WTO obligations invoked in these proceedings. In this respect, the panel found in all four reports that the US had acted inconsistently with obligations incumbent on it under the GATT (e.g. Article I (most-favoured nation treatment) and Article II (tariff bindings) in the case brought by China).[135]

Next the panel had to address a central issue, namely the relationship between Article XIX of the GATT, the Safeguards Agreement and Article XXI of the GATT. This was necessary given that the complainants in all four proceedings had claimed that the US had infringed several of its obligations under the Safeguards Agreement, which establishes rules for the application of Article XIX of the GATT that permits WTO Members to restrict trade if, as a result of unforeseen developments, certain products are imported in such quantities as to cause or threaten serious injury to domestic producers. In response, the US argued that Article XIX and the Safeguards Agreement have simply become inapplicable, since it had invoked the security exception enshrined in Article XXI of the GATT. Hence, the panel was called upon to interpret Article 11(1)(c) of the Safeguards Agreement, which explicitly regulates the relationship between this agreement and the GATT by stipulating in relevant part that "[t]his Agreement does not apply to measures sought, taken or maintained by a Member pursuant to provisions of GATT 1994 other than Article XIX".

The panel expressed the view that the wording "*pursuant to* provisions of the GATT" does not mean that a Member's measure must be "in conformity with" such provisions, but merely requires that the measure is taken under a GATT provision other than Article XIX.[136] Given that the panel found that a "central aspect of the design and application" of the US measures was their relation to the US' determination of a threat to its national security, the panel concluded that the US measures were indeed taken "pursuant to" Article XXI of the GATT. Consequently, the Safeguards Agreement was found to be inapplicable.[137]

Regarding this systemic issue of the relationship between Article XIX of the GATT and the Safeguards Agreement on the one hand and Article XXI of the GATT on the other hand, it should be emphasized that the panel's approach does not effectively open the door for circumventions of Article XIX and the Safeguards Agreement: even though the panel's stance results in the inapplicability of the WTO disciplines on safeguard measures, whenever a WTO Member argues that its

[135] Panel report, *US – Steel (China)*, para 8.1.

[136] Panel report, *US – Steel (China)*, paras 7.62 ff.

[137] Panel report, *US – Steel (China)*, paras 7.82 ff (quotation at para 7.96).

measures have been taken for reasons of national security, the panel has virtually barred the gate for obvious attempts of escaping GATT disciplines by opting for strict scrutiny under Article XXI(b)(iii) of the GATT as will be seen in the next section.

3.6.3 *Interpretation and Substantive Assessment*

As respects the panel's approach to Article XXI(b), it is conspicuous that it has not at all referred to the preceding panel report in *Russia – Transit*, although the latter had been expected by trade experts to serve as a model for future reports,[138] nor to the report in *Saudi Arabia – IPRs*.[139]

In the *US – Steel* proceedings, the US had claimed that its "invocation of Article XXI is a non-justiciable issue as Article XXI makes its invocation self-judging by the Member taking the security action".[140] It had tried to further clarify its stance by stating that "the United States is not requesting that the Panel refrain from applying the rules and procedures of the DSU".[141] Rather, as indicated above, it argued that the panel should limit its findings to recognizing that Article XXI(b) had been invoked.[142] Since, in the US view, Article XXI is "self-judging", the only requirement for the Member invoking it "is for the Member to consider that a particular action is necessary to protect its essential security interests in any of the circumstances identified in Article XXI(b)". This means, according to the US, that this requirement is met "once the Member indicates [. . .] that it has made such a determination".[143]

As explained by the panel, the US claim relies on the premise, already advanced by Russia in the *Russia – Transit* case, that the wording "it considers" in the Chapeau of Article XXI(b) does not only qualify the Chapeau, but also the subparagraphs of Article XXI(b). Adopting a self-standing approach to this issue, the panel turned to an extensive interpretation of Article XXI(b), relying on elaborate grammatical considerations, the principle of effective interpretation, relevant context and the object and purpose of the GATT and the WTO Agreement more generally. On this basis, the panel concluded first that the right to take action under Article XXI (b) "consists of an express provision of *deference*" under the Chapeau,[144] which, however, is complemented by the three subparagraphs of Article XXI(b) that set out

[138] Cf. e.g. Van den Bossche and Zdouc (2022), p. 675.

[139] One exception being fn 479, where the *US – Steel* panel distinguished part of its order analysis from the two preceding reports.

[140] Panel report, *US – Steel (China)*, para 7.2.

[141] Panel report, *US – Steel (China)*, para 7.3.

[142] See above, Sect. 3.1.

[143] Panel report, *US – Steel (China)*, para 7.105.

[144] Panel report, *US – Steel (China)*, para 7.122 (italics added).

objective conditions for the exercise of this right. On the basis of this interpretive result, which is in line with the panel report in *Russia – Transit*, the panel rejected the US claim that Article XXI(b) is "self-judging" in the sense of being "non-justiciable".[145]

The panel then turned to the interpretation of the third subparagraph of Article XXI(b). Starting out from dictionary definitions, the panel first found that the "the term 'emergency' includes '[a] situation, esp. of danger or conflict, that arises unexpectedly and requires urgent attention', 'a condition requiring immediate treatment', or a 'pressing need'." Due to the wording "emergency in *international relations*", the panel held that "an emergency in purely domestic or national affairs" would not be covered by this provision.[146] Due to the fact that the term "war" is situated next to the phrase "emergency in international relations" and based on contextual and teleological arguments, the panel concluded that an emergency in the sense of Article XXI(b)(iii) "must be, if not equally grave or severe, at least comparable in its gravity or severity to a 'war' in terms of its impact on international relations".[147] Hence, the panel clearly emphasized the nexus between "emergency in international relations" and military conflicts.

Finally, the panel reviewed the evidence and arguments submitted in this dispute. It found, *inter alia*, that part of this evidence showed that the US consideration that its national security was threatened was based on factors which focused "predominantly on developments relating to the domestic situation of steel and aluminium industries in the United States".[148] Furthermore, the panel held that some of the evidence pertained to domestic legal standards and could not be directly transposed to the assessment required under WTO law. Moreover, the panel also took into account evidence submitted by the US relating to a global excess capacity in steel and aluminium, which, as the panel acknowledged, "ha[d] been raised as a matter of international attention within the conduct of international relations of various countries".[149] However, the panel concluded that the evidence and arguments submitted were not sufficient to persuade it that the situation at issue "rises to the gravity or severity of tensions on the international plane so as to constitute an 'emergency in international relations' during which a Member may act under Article XXI(b)(iii)".[150] Consequently, the panel found that the US infringements of the GATT were not justified under Article XXI(b)(iii).[151]

[145] Panel report, *US – Steel (China)*, paras 7.122–7.128 (quotations at para 7.128; italics added).

[146] Panel report, *US – Steel (China)*, para 7.137.

[147] Panel report, *US – Steel (China)*, para 7.139–7.141 (quotation at para 7.139).

[148] Panel report, *US – Steel (China)*, para 7.142.

[149] Panel report, *US – Steel (China)*, paras 7.143 ff (quotation at para 7.147).

[150] Panel report, *US – Steel (China)*, para 7.148.

[151] Panel report, *US – Steel (China)*, para 7.149.

Overall, as expected in view of the panel report in *Russia – Transit*,[152] the US could not successfully rely on Article XXI of the GATT in order to justify its trade restrictions.

3.7 Interim Conclusions in Comparative Perspective

As has become evident in the preceding sections, the approaches of the panels in the disputes in *Russia – Transit*, *Saudi Arabia – IPRs* and *US – Steel* differed considerably as regards the order of analysis adopted and their assessment of the criteria in Article XXI of the GATT and Article 73 of the TRIPS Agreement. Therefore, the main conclusions of these reports shall be briefly summarized in comparative perspective in this section.

- First, as regards the question of a panel's **jurisdiction** under Article XXI of the GATT and Article 73 of the TRIPS Agreement as well as the issue of the justiciability of disputes in which these security exceptions are invoked, the panels had to grapple with diverging understandings, by the litigants and third parties in these disputes, of the concept of "**self-judging**" clauses.
  - In this context, the panel in *Russia – Transit* has found that it has jurisdiction in disputes in which Article XXI is invoked, in particular in view of the fact that the DSU contains no special rules for proceedings involving Article XXI.
  - Similarly, the panel in *Saudi Arabia – IPRs* held that the DSU does not grant panels discretion to decline to exercise their jurisdiction, which has in principle been established in conformity with the DSU, if a security exception is invoked.
  - Furthermore, the panel in the 2022 *US – Steel* reports found that the mere invocation of the GATT security exception does not make a matter "**non-justiciable**" in the sense of making it legally impossible for panels to make findings under the substantive provisions of WTO law.
- Secondly, the panels in *Russia – Transit* and *US – Steel* explicitly regarded the **subparagraphs** of the GATT and TRIPS security exceptions as objective limitative clauses in the sense of preconditions that must be fulfilled, before the Chapeaus of these exceptions—and the discretion granted to WTO Members under these Chapeaus—can be invoked.
- Thirdly, a low **burden of proof** has been placed on the respondents in the panel reports in *Russia – Transit* and *Saudi – Arabia* as regards the **existence of the situation** which had been claimed by the respondents to constitute an emergency in international law. This issue has not been discussed in detail in *US – Steel*.

[152] On this cf. Van den Bossche and Akpofure (2020).

- Fourthly, the criterion "**emergency in international relations**" has been **defined** by the *Russia – Transit* panel as encompassing "defence and military interests, as well as maintenance of law and public order interests"; mere political or economic differences have not been regarded as being "sufficient, of themselves" to constitute such an emergency.
  - Moreover, an "emergency in international relations" was understood to mean "a situation of armed conflict, or of latent armed conflict, or of heightened tension or crisis, or of general instability engulfing or surrounding a state" in *Russia – Transit.* The panel in *Saudi – Arabia* concurred with this definition, which puts considerable constraints on this criterion.
  - While this definition could possibly be read as covering e.g. severe economic concerns that raise "maintenance of law or public order interests", the panel in *US – Steel* explicitly required that an "emergency in international relations" must "at least [be] **comparable** in its gravity or severity **to a 'war'** in terms of its impact on international relations" and **excluded** purely domestic or national emergencies from the scope of the security exception.
- Fifthly, the term "**taken in time of**" an emergency in international relations has been interpreted in both *Russia – Transit* and *Saudi Arabia – IPRs* as requiring that the measures to be justified must be taken "during" the emergency at issue.
- Sixthly, the concept of "**essential security interests**" in the Chapeau of Article XXI(b) of the GATT has been defined as "generally [referring to] interests relating to the quintessential functions" of a state in *Russia – Transit*, which has also granted **broad discretion** to WTO Members, leaving it "in general" to them to define their essential security interests.
  - This discretion has, however, been regarded by the panel as being constrained by the principle of **good faith**, according to which WTO Members must not invoke security interests in order to circumvent their obligations under WTO law, but must articulate their essential security interests sufficiently enough to demonstrate their "veracity".
  - In this context, the panel adopted a **"sliding scale" approach**, according to which "the further removed" a situation is from an armed conflict, the greater the burden argumentation will be for the state invoking the security exception under the GATT.
  - In contrast, the panel in *Saudi Arabia – IPRs* understood the criterion of essential security interests merely as a benchmark for assessing the measures taken by the Member invoking the security exception in the TRIPS Agreement and did neither adopt the "veracity" test, nor apply the sliding scale approach introduced in *Russia – Transit.*
  - In contradistinction with *Russia – Transit*, the *Saudi Arabia – IPRs* panel applied the requirement of "sufficient articulation" to the "link" between the means adopted and the security interests pursued by the respondent party.
- Seventhly, regarding this **nexus** between ends and means, the panels in both *Russia – Transit* and *Saudi Arabia – IPRs* merely required that it is **not**

"implausible" that the measures imposed by the respondent have been taken for the protection of its essential security interests.

- Eighthly, the phrase **"it considers"** in the Chapeau, which has been the focus of academic and political debates for several decades, has been interpreted by both panels as relating to the question as to whether the actions taken by the respondent are **"necessary"**. Strikingly, this has led the panel in *Russia – Transit* to conclude that the assessment of the necessity of the measures taken is left to the respondent WTO Member. In contrast, the panel in *Saudi Arabia – IPRs* has related the plausibility test to the necessity requirement and seems to have at least implicitly applied it in the concrete case.
- Finally, as respects the relationship between Article XIX of the GATT, the WTO Safeguards Agreement and Article XXI of the GATT, the panel in *US – Steel* has held that the **Safeguards Agreement** does not apply to measures taken by a WTO Member "pursuant to" Article XXI of the GATT, irrespective of whether such a measure is "in conformity" with this provision.

References

Akande D, Williams S (2003) International adjudication on national security issues: what role for the WTO? Virginia J Int Law 43:365–404

Alford RR (2011) The self-judging WTO security exception. Utah Law Rev 3:697–759

Arato J, Claussen K, Heath B (2020) The perils of pandemic exceptionalism. Am J Int Law 114(4): 627–636

Bogdanova I (2021) Targeted economic sanctions and WTO law. Leg Issues Econ Integr 48(2): 171–200

Boklan D, Bahri A (2020) The first WTO's ruling on national security exception. World Trade

Cohen HG (2020) Nations and markets. J Int Econ Law 23:793–815

Collins D (2022) The WTO's essential security exception and revocation of Russia's most favoured nation status following the invasion of Ukraine. City Law Forum, 15 March 2022. https://blogs.city.ac.uk/citylawforum/2022/03/15/the-wtos-essential-security-exception-and-revocation-of-russias-most-favoured-nation-status-following-the-invasion-of-ukraine. Accessed 4 Jan 2023

Gladysz J (2021) The national security exception in WTO law: emerging jurisprudence and future direction. Georgetown J Int Law 52:835–861

Glöckle C (2019) Nationale Sicherheitsinteressen in Russia-traffic in transit. Europäische Zeitschrift für Wirtschaftsrecht 15:652–659

Hahn MJ (1991) Vital interests and the law of the GATT: an analysis of GATT's security exception. Mich J Int Law 12(3):558–620

Hahn MJ (1996) Die einseitige Aussetzung von GATT-Verpflichtungen als Repressalie. Springer, Berlin

Heath JB (2020) Trade and security among the ruins. Duke J Comp Int Law 30:223–266

Kolb R (2017) Good faith in international law. Hart, Oxford

Mantilla Blanco S, Pehl A (2020) National security exceptions in international trade and investment agreements. Justiciability and standards of review. Springer, Cham

Milanov M (2021) A Lauterpachtian affair: security exceptions as 'self-judging obligations' in the case law of the International Court of Justice and beyond. J World Invest Trade 22:509–560

Paulsen M (2022) Characterizing war in a trade context. Opinio Juris, 10 March 2022. https://opiniojuris.org/2022/03/10/characterizing-war-in-a-trade-context. Accessed 4 Jan 2023

Ranjan P (2022) Russia-Ukraine war and WTO's national security exception. Foreign Trade Review, Online First. https://journals.sagepub.com/doi/full/10.1177/00157325221114586. Accessed 4 Jan 2023

Roberts A, Choer Moraes H, Ferguson V (2019) Toward a geoeconomic order in international trade and investment. J Int Econ Law 22:655–676

Schill S, Briese R (2009) "If the state considers": self-judging clauses in international dispute settlement. In: von Bogdandy A, Wolfrum R (eds) Max Planck Yearbook of United Nations Law, vol 13, pp 61–140

Schloemann HL, Ohlhoff S (1999) Constitutionalization and dispute settlement in the WTO: national security as an issue of competence. Am J Int Law 93:424–451

Van den Bossche P, Akpofure S (2020) The use and abuse of the national security exception under Article XXI(b)(iii) of the GATT 1994. WTI working paper no. 03/2020. https://www.wti.org/research/publications/1299/the-use-and-abuse-of-the-national-security-exception-under-article-xxibiii-of-the-gatt-1994. Accessed 4 Jan 2023

Van den Bossche P, Zdouc W (2022) The law and policy of the World Trade Organization, 5th edn. Cambridge University Press, Cambridge

Vidigal G (2019) WTO adjudication and the security exception: something old, something new, something borrowed – something blue? Leg Issues Econ Integr 46(3):203–224

Vranes E (2009) Trade and the environment. Fundamental issues in international law, WTO law, and legal theory. Oxford University Press, Oxford

Weiß W (2020) Adjudicating security exceptions in WTO law: methodical and procedural preliminaries. J World Trade 54(6):829–852

Zhou J (2020) New WTO ruling on national security in Qatar-Saudi Arabia case and its impact on South Korea-Japan dispute. ASIL Insights 24(22), 3 September 2020. https://www.asil.org/insights/volume/24/issue/22/new-wto-ruling-national-security-qatar-saudi-arabia-case-and-its-impact. Accessed 4 Jan 2023

Chapter 4
Methodological Aspects: Curtailing "Trump Cards" Through Good Faith and Proportionality?

As ensues from the preceding analysis, the WTO panel reports having dealt with the WTO security exceptions so far have clarified central issues pertaining to their interpretation. Several unclarities still need elucidation in future reports, however. Moreover, although there meanwhile is a considerable amount of case studies examining in particular the ruling in *Russia – Transit*, a central issue still requires further clarification: that is the question as to how the review under the Chapeau, in particular under the standard of good faith, is to be concretized.

One quite elaborate theory has been proposed by *Schill* and *Briese*. This approach will be examined in the next section. The remaining sections of this chapter will then argue that the review of good faith under the Chapeau of the WTO security exceptions should be concretized by the principle of proportionality.

4.1 Analogy with National Administrative Law?

As mentioned above, in their seminal article on "self-judging clauses", *Schill* and *Briese* start out from the premise that most authors and international tribunals concur that such clauses do not oust the jurisdiction of international tribunals, but affect the standard of review to be applied. While they envisage to propose a "general standard of review" of self-judging clauses,[1] they address Article XXI of the GATT as a principal example. According to *Schill* and *Briese*, it is mostly held by international tribunals and scholars alike that the standard of review applied under such clauses is review for good faith. They therefore concentrate on the question as to how good faith review can be concretized in a manner which neither attributes unduly broad powers to tribunals on the one hand, nor leaves too much discretion to states subject

[1] Schill and Briese (2009), p. 120 ("Towards a General Standard of Review for Self-Judging Clauses").

E. Vranes, *WTO Security Exceptions in Practice and Scholarship*, SpringerBriefs in Law, https://doi.org/10.1007/978-3-031-36702-1_4

to such review on the other hand.[2] In this regard, they suggest, "as a useful approach", to draw an analogy with the standard of review applied by domestic courts reviewing discretionary decision-making by administrative bodies.[3]

In order to explain the plausibility of their approach, they argue that "state action on the international level increasingly resembles administrative action" in domestic contexts.[4] *Schill* and *Briese* therefore undertake a comparative overview of administrative review in countries in the Common Law system, the US, France and Germany. They summarize their findings as implying that domestic judicial review of administrative decision-making in these countries emphasizes formal and procedural control mechanisms, with tribunals reviewing "whether the factual basis of the administration's decision was adequate and properly investigated, whether the appreciation of the legal framework was correct, whether the administrative agency abided by the proper procedure and whether it was guided in the exercise of discretion by relevant and pertinent considerations".[5] They conclude that domestic courts in these legal systems focus on formal issues such as the right to be heard, lack of bias, sufficient and transparent reasoning, consistency and non-discriminatory decision-making. Moreover, they refer to the fact that proportionality review is increasingly applied in many domestic and international dispute settlement systems, emphasizing that "disproportionality may be a factor suggesting a lack of good faith".[6]

On the basis of their analogy argument, *Schill* and *Briese* submit that international courts, like domestic judges, should "first isolate the elements of a treaty provision that are self-judging". Regarding such elements, judicial review should concentrate on "procedural grounds of review", which means that it should be examined whether the state invoking such a clause has "misused its discretionary powers". According to *Schill* and *Briese*, this ought to include an examination as to whether the factual basis of the decision has been adequately investigated, whether the applicable legal rules have been correctly assessed, whether procedural requirements have been complied with, whether the exercise of discretion has abided by relevant considerations, and whether other contracting parties have been properly informed about relevant reasons. Moreover, the purpose of the self-judging clause and the treaty framework should be taken into account.[7]

It is to be underlined that *Schill* and *Briese* have indeed predicted parts of the reasoning meanwhile adopted by the panels in *Russia – Transit*, *Saudi Arabia – IPRs* and *US – Steel.* It is conspicuous, however, that the reasoning of these panels relies on arguments developed under international law and WTO law and have not been derived, *per analogiam*, from national law. On the more concrete methodological

[2] Schill and Briese (2009), p. 120.

[3] Schill and Briese (2009), pp. 120–121.

[4] Schill and Briese (2009), p. 125.

[5] Schill and Briese (2009), p. 134.

[6] Schill and Briese (2009), pp. 134–135.

[7] Schill and Briese (2009), pp. 136–138.

level of the interpretation of "self-judging clauses" like Article XXI of the GATT it can also be questioned whether such analogies with national law—if conceivable—are necessary at all. Thus, it seems doubtful e.g. whether the requirement that international tribunals should "first isolate the elements of a treaty provision that are self-judging" needs an analogy with national law. It is submitted that it follows from the evident duty of judges to correctly apply the law (and related methodological requirements of adequate interpretation) that judges need to inquire into the meaning of applicable norms and the standard of review required under such norms. Similarly, there seems to be no need for an analogy with national law for arguing that international tribunals should examine whether a state invoking "self-judging" clauses has "misused its discretionary powers": does it not follow from the prohibition on abuse of law (which can be regarded as the reverse side of the medal of good faith)[8] that norms must not be misused or circumvented? It is noteworthy that in this concrete respect, too, the panel in *Russia – Transit* has achieved the same result on the basis of international law and the interpretation of the applicable norms of WTO law,[9] without having seen the need to resort to analogies with national law.

Likewise, as regards the opinion that good faith review should include an inquiry into whether the factual basis has been adequately investigated by the state invoking a security exception such as Article XXI does not seem to require an analogy with national law. This result has been reached by the panels in the *Russia – Transit*, *Saudi Arabia – IPRs* and *US – Steel* cases, too, without such analogy: this is evident e.g. in the context of their inquiries into whether the situation, which was claimed by the respondents as amounting to an emergency in international relations, really existed.[10]

Regarding Article XXI of the GATT, there also seems to be no need for drawing analogies with national law as respects the issues of whether the (domestic) applicable legal rules have been correctly assessed, whether relevant procedural requirements have been complied with, whether the exercise of discretion has abided by relevant considerations, whether national rules have been applied consistently and impartially, and whether other contracting parties have been properly informed about relevant reasons for the imposition of the measures at issue: in the GATT context, these requirements, which can indeed be seen as concretizations of good faith, are largely covered by Article X of the GATT[11] and have been held, by the

---

[8]See e.g. the Appellate Body report, *US – Shrimp*, para 158.

[9]Panel report, *Russia – Transit*, paras 7.132–7.133, where the panel, referring to Appellate Body rulings, argued: "...the discretion of a Member to designate particular concerns as 'essential security interests' is limited by its obligation to interpret and apply Article XXI(b)(iii) of the GATT 1994 in good faith. The Panel recalls that the obligation of good faith is a general principle of law and a principle of general international law which underlies all treaties, as codified in Article 31(1)...of the Vienna Convention" (para 7.132) and concluded that "[t]he obligation of good faith requires that Members not use the exceptions in Article XXI as a means to *circumvent* their obligations under the GATT 1994" (para 7.133, italics added).

[10]See above, Sect. 3.4.3.

[11]Cf. e.g. Van den Bossche and Zdouc (2022), pp. 544 ff.

Appellate Body, to apply *a fortiori* when a WTO Member tries to justify contraventions of WTO law.[12] Finally, the requirement, also derived *per analogiam* from national law by *Schill* and *Briese*, to take into account the purpose of a "self-judging clause" and the purpose of the relevant treaty framework arguably does not need such analogy for the obvious reason that this requirement of systematic-teleological interpretation follows from international law and legal methodology.

In sum, it is submitted that a "theoretical" approach to the concretization of the Chapeau and the good faith standard encompassed by it should be inferred from the relevant normative structures of international law and WTO law themselves. We will turn to this issue in the next sections.

4.2 Proportionality as a Concretization of Good Faith

In the following we will focus on XXI(b)(iii) of the GATT, which, as has been explained above, is the central clause in the security exception of the GATT. The following considerations are of course also relevant for the virtually identical security exceptions laid down in Article 73(b)(iii) of the TRIPS Agreement and Article XIV*bis*(1)(b)(iii) of the GATS. By implication, they may also be helpful in the interpretation of clauses in other international agreements that have been modelled upon Article XXI of the GATT.

As has been argued in the literature, Article XXI is "all about balancing":[13] it is clearly concerned with balancing economic and security interests, but is also about balancing unilateralism and multilateralism, the roles of judges and politics, international governance and national decision-making, and the role of the market versus the state.[14] The panel reports reviewed in this study, too, have clearly conceived of Article XXI of the GATT and Article 73 of the TRIPS Agreement as means for finding the appropriate balance between competing rights and interests. In this respect, they have regarded the principle of good faith as the standard guiding their review.

The crucial question, as indicated above, is how this review can be operationalized, i.e. how the vague concept of "good faith" can be applied to concrete cases or classes of similar cases. Indeed, there is a clear need for structuring this review in order to increase the transparency—and thereby rationality—of argumentation. The relevant criteria have to be inferred—and this is the crucial point—from international law and the applicable norms and structures of WTO law.

---

[12] Cf. the Appellate Body Report in *US – Shrimp*, paras 178–183, referring to the "general exceptions" clause of Article XX of the GATT.

[13] Mantilla Blanco and Pehl (2020), p. 26.

[14] Cf. e.g. Schill and Briese (2009), p. 62.

In the following, it will be submitted that the principle of good faith, which underlies *all* treaty obligations, should be concretized, or "operationalized", in the *concrete* context of the Chapeau of Article XXI(b)(iii) through the principle of proportionality both for reasons of international and WTO on the one hand law and legal methodology on the other hand. In this regard, we will proceed as follows: In the next subsection, we will once more take a short look at the relevant structures of Article XXI(b)(iii). We will then turn to the legal status of the principle of proportionality and will explain that the principle of proportionality is inherent in systematic-teleological interpretation. This also holds true for the subtests of the proportionality principle in the broad sense, i.e. the subtests of suitability, necessity and proportionality in the strict sense, which are often associated with this concept and serve to structure argumentation and increase transparency.[15] Finally, these considerations will be applied to Article XXI(b)(iii).

4.2.1 *The Structure of Article XXI(b)(iii): Ends and Means, Rule Versus Exception*

As has been emphasized by various authors and the ICJ alike, Article XXI clearly has to be understood as an exception to the rule,[16] the obvious "rule" in this context being the requirement to comply with the obligations undertaken by WTO Members under the GATT, the "exception" being the possibility to deviate from these obligations under the conditions laid down in Article XXI.

Article XXI(b)(iii) as the central provision in Article XXI is clearly concerned with (i) the *aims* pursued by a WTO Member invoking this exception, (ii) the *measures* employed and (iii) the *relationship between* these aims and measures. In other words, Article XXI(b)(iii) deals with (i) ends, (ii) means and (iii) the relationship between ends and means. Moreover, it is explicitly concerned (iv) with the standard of review to be applied and lays down (v and vi) preconditions for invoking this exception.

For more clarity, this can be illustrated as follows:

[15] See below, Sect. 4.2.2.1.

[16] Hahn (1991), pp. 578 ff; the ICJ held that Article XXI "contemplate[s] exceptions to the normal implementation of the General Agreement" (ICJ, Military and Paramilitary Activities in and against Nicaragua, ICJ Reports 1986, 14 ff, para 222 (on this see e.g. Schill and Briese (2009), pp. 69 ff)). Similarly, Mantilla Blanco and Pehl (2020), p. 10 have referred to the "exceptional character" of Article XXI.

- **Chapeau**:

(i)	"essential security interests"	⇔	*ends*
(ii)	"any action"	⇔	*means*
(iii)	"necessary"	⇔	*ends – means relationship*
(iv)	"it considers"	⇔	standard of review

- **subparagraph (iii):**

(v)	"taken in time of"	⇔	precondition
(vi)	"emergency in intl. rel."	⇔	precondition

As already indicated, the proportionality principle can be seen as being inherent both in systematic-teleological interpretation in particular in rule vs exception constellations as well as in the interplay between (legal) ends and means. In the following, this will be explained in more detail (see below, Sect. 4.2.2.1.1). However, given that the legal status of the principle of proportionality is disputed in international law according to some authors, we need to address this issue first.

4.2.2 The Legal Status of the Proportionality Principle[17]

Some authors have argued that the application of the WTO security exceptions in general and the good faith review under Article XXI of the GATT in particular should comprise a proportionality review.[18] Yet, as this has not been elaborated in more detail in the literature so far, we will try to do so in the following.

It is conspicuous that the legal status of the principle of proportionality is disputed in international law. On the one hand, the principle of proportionality is sometimes characterized as a general principle of law,[19] as a general principle of international law[20] and as being recognized in universal customary international law.[21] It is frequently recognized as being embodied in the principles of reprisal,[22] self-help,

[17] This subsection draws on Vranes (2009), pp. 129–154 and 256–282.

[18] Cf. Heath (2020), pp. 256 ff, referring to arguments in academic literature, pleadings of some WTO Members and dicta of some investment tribunals concerning similar security exceptions; see also Schloemann and Ohlhoff (1999), pp. 444–445; Schill and Briese (2009), pp. 106 ff; Akande and Williams (2003), p. 399; see also Van den Bossche and Akpofure (2020), text at fn 156.

[19] Cf. Delbrück (1997), p. 1144.

[20] Cf. Delbrück (1997), p. 1144; Bleckmann (1995), p. 680; Mosler (1976), p. 45; Hilf and Puth (2002), pp. 210–211.

[21] Hilf and Puth (2002), p. 209.

[22] Cf. Dicke (1978), p. 181; Delbrück (1997), p. 1142.

in Article 60 VCLT,[23] and in humanitarian law.[24] Further, the principle of proportionality is seen by some authors as forming part of WTO rules.[25]

On the other hand, however, although several writers refer to the notion of "proportionality", there seems to be no uniform understanding on its contents or structures. Notably, it has to be stressed that writers often do not refer to the three-tier test known in especially from legal theory, EU law and various domestic legal systems,[26] which comprises the tests of suitability, necessity and proportionality in the narrow sense[27] (these subtests will be discussed in the following[28]). Furthermore, there are authors who claim that the principle is not inherent in the international legal order and could not be transposed to international law, even if it existed in all states, for lack of uniformity.[29]

In other words, the existence, foundations and functions of the principle of proportionality are still contested in international law, although the idea of proportionality, and the closely associated concept of balancing principles, values and interests, have in fact occupied a cardinal place in philosophy and legal thinking

---

[23] On all of this cf. also Krugmann (2004), pp. 15 ff; Bockslaff (1987), p. 137 with further references.

[24] Cf. Bockslaff (1987), p. 137, who refers to Art 35, 51(5) b, 54, 56, 57, 85, 90 of the Protocol Additional to the Geneva Conventions of 12 August 1949, and relating to the Protection of Victims of International Armed Conflicts (Protocol 1), adopted on 8 June 1977 (available at http://www.unhchr.ch/html/menu3/b/93.htm).

[25] See e.g. Hilf and Puth (2002), pp. 199 ff. Moreover, according to Jenks (1958), pp. 139–143, the principle of proportionality is recognized as governing the legality of self-defence in all civil law systems, Islamic, Hindu, Jewish, Chinese and African Law. Furthermore, notions such as "necessary", "excessive in relation to", "proportional" and "appropriate", which are often associated with the proportionality principle, can be found in a series of international treaties (cf. e.g. Art 12, 18, 19, 21, 22 of the International Covenant on Civil and Political Rights (available at http://www.ohchr.org/english/law/ccpr.htm); Art 8–11 ECHR; on this cf. also Krugmann (2004), pp. 13–14; Hilf and Puth (2002), pp. 199 ff). The principle of proportionality has also been referred to in international decisions e.g. on continental shelf disputes (ICJ, *North Sea Continental Shelf Cases* (Germany, Netherlands, Denmark) judgment of 20 February 1969; ICJ, *Case Concerning the Continental Shelf* (Tunisia, Libyan Arab Jamahiriya) judgment of 3 June 1985, paras 74 ff; see also the arbitration on the delimitation of the continental shelf between the United Kingdom and France, discussed by Klemm (1981), pp. 58 ff), where it has been understood as an instrument for balancing state interests (for an overview cf. also Koskenniemi (1990), pp. 14 ff).

[26] For comparative overviews cf. Barak (2012); Stone Sweet and Mathews (2008), pp. 72 ff; Mathews and Stone Sweet (2011), p. 797; Cohen-Eliya and Porat (2010), pp. 263 ff; Vranes (2017), pp. 99 ff.

[27] Cf. Krugmann (2004), p. 13. For example, the principle has been characterized as a substantive norm by Bockslaff (1987), pp. 142–146 ("*individuell-substantielle Regel*", "*materielle Ausgleichsnorm*"), which is at odds with the understanding in legal theory at least, which regards the principle as a purely formal framework for rational argumentation. The same holds true for Krugmann's study that is devoted to the principle of proportionality in international law and designates proportionality as a principle that has to be given substantive contents, which needs not necessarily be subdivided into the three-tier test just referred to (Krugmann (2004), pp. 11–13).

[28] Cf. below, Sect. 4.2.2.2.

[29] Dicke (1978), p. 181.

since the beginning of occidental philosophy.[30] Therefore, this section will first examine its legal status in more detail.

4.2.2.1 Proportionality: General Principle of Law, Interpretative Principle, or Maxim of Rational Decision-Making?

Even those writers who consider that the principle of proportionality forms part of the international legal order commonly admit that its contents are disputed.[31] It may be helpful, therefore, to adopt the approach of several writers on the subject who refer to the principle of proportionality, as it is known from EU law and several national legal systems,[32] as a model against which further considerations can be compared. In these legal orders, the principle of proportionality is understood as comprising three sub-principles or subtests which serve to reconcile competing rights: First, a measure adopted in pursuit of a legitimate goal must be *suitable* to promote this aim; second, it must represent the means which is least violative of the competing right, otherwise it is deemed not *necessary*; third, the benefits of pursuing the legitimate aim must not be out of proportion to the extent to which the competing right is restricted. These subtests are usually designated as the requirements of suitability, necessity and proportionality in the narrow sense. Suitability is also referred to as effectiveness in this context; the subtest of proportionality in the narrow sense is sometimes also referred to as balancing.[33,34] In the following, the notion "principle of proportionality in the broad sense" will be employed to refer to the overall test encompassing these three requirements, when this is necessary to distinguish it from the principle of proportionality in the narrow sense.

The principle of proportionality is frequently portrayed as having its "modern"[35] origins in German law, more precisely in Prussian law governing the activities of

[30] Thus, while maxims such as "*ne quid nimis*", "*pan métron ariston*" and "*nichts im Übermaß*" are central to *Socrates*, *Platon*, *Cicero* and later philosophers, *Solon* had already made the maxim of not pursuing aims with disproportionate means a leading principle of legislation. On this cf. Ottmann (1980), pp. 808 ff; see also Wieacker (1979), pp. 874 ff; Medicus (1992), pp. 35 ff; Tridimas (1999), pp. 65 ff; Delbrück (1984), p. 396. For a more comprehensive discussion and further references see also Vranes (2017), pp. 99 ff.

[31] Cf. e.g. Delbrück (1997), pp. 1143–1144; Hilf and Puth (2002), pp. 209 ff.

[32] See e.g. Barak (2012); Stone Sweet and Mathews (2008), pp. 72 ff; Mathews and Stone Sweet (2011), p. 797; Cohen-Eliya and Porat (2010), pp. 263 ff; Vranes (2017), pp. 99 ff.

[33] From the vast amount of literature regarding EU law, cf. e.g. the contributions in Ellis (1999) (in particular Jacobs (1999), p. 1; van Gerven (1999), p. 37; Tridimas (1999), p. 65; Craig (1999), p. 85); see also Jans (2000), p. 239; Neumann and Türk (2003), pp. 201 ff with further references on EU law.

[34] Regarding German law, cf. in particular Hirschberg (1981), pp. 43 ff and 50 ff; Holoubek (1995), pp. 97 ff.

[35] Hilf and Puth (2002), pp. 200 ff.

police authorities,[36] from where it has allegedly been "transposed" to EU law,[37] international law and WTO law.[38] Other writers, however, regard the subtests as being derived from the concept of law.[39] A third group of writers consider these principles as maxims of interpretation or as necessary maxims of rational decision-making more generally.[40] These views arguably imply a weaker, but at the same time broader status.

For the purposes of this study, we will focus on the third view.

4.2.2.1.1 The Three Subtests as Interpretative Principles Following from the "Logic of Ends and Means" and the Interplay Between Rule and Exception

According to *Röhl* and *Röhl*, the three requirements encompassed by the proportionality principle in the broad sense form part of *teleological interpretation*. In their view, the structure of the proportionality principle can be seen as flowing from the "logic of ends (*telos*) and means": Means incur costs as they have side-effects; therefore, adopting a means that is not suitable for promoting a legitimate purpose is impermissible if it harms other legitimate purposes (test of suitability). In order to minimize costs, only the means least violative of concurrent legitimate interests should be employed (test of necessity). Even the mildest means may still be disproportionate if it impinges excessively on another one's legitimate interests: this again mandates that the interests pursued be evaluated and compared in the concrete case (test of proportionality in the narrow sense).[41] In this view, the principle of proportionality and its three subtests do not actually function as a legal principle, but as *interpretative maxims*. Together, the subtests form a method of *rationally balancing values*, which is regarded as being "applicable in any given legal field".[42]

One could also express this in the terminology of a "logic of rule and exception": if a given norm is clearly instituted as expressing a fundamental rule in a given context, while another norm constitutes a limited exception, it is quite evident that means that are *unsuitable* to promote the purpose of the exception are excluded by the interplay of rule and exception; further, only the means least violative of the rule will normally be acceptable as being *necessary* under the exception; and finally *disproportionate* means cannot normally be regarded as being covered, or "justified", by the exception.

---

[36] Cf. e.g. Hirschberg (1981), pp. 1 ff.

[37] Cf. e.g. Holoubek (1995), pp. 97 ff; Hilf and Puth (2002), p. 199.

[38] For a critical review of these views cf. Vranes (2017), pp. 99 ff with further references.

[39] Cf. below, Sect. 4.2.2.1.2.

[40] Cf. below, Sects. 4.2.2.1.1 and 4.2.2.1.3.

[41] Cf. Röhl and Röhl (2008), pp. 620 ff and 655 ff.

[42] Röhl and Röhl (2008), pp. 620 ff and 655 ff.

These approaches underline that the three-tier structure plausibly follows from the "normal" method of *systematic-teleological interpretation*, in particular in rule vs exception constellations. Hence, resorting to the terminology of proportionality, balancing and the disputed model of "principles" in a *Dworkian* or post-*Dworkian* sense, which is often seen as being linked with the proportionality principle,[43] may be illustrative. It is not indispensable, however.

4.2.2.1.2 The Subtests as Flowing from the Concept of Law

On the other hand, *Wieacker* has argued that the principle of proportionality has its firmest root in the fundamental idea of utility of law, according to which law is but a *means* that has to serve human *purposes*. This view comes close to the "logic of ends and means" and teleological interpretation addressed in the preceding section: according to *Wieacker*, this relation between ends and means is characterized by the requirements of *necessity* and *proportionality* in its narrow sense, the pivotal point being what he calls economic principle (*Ökonomiegebot*).[44,45] But for the test of suitability (which is quite self-evident), this reasoning leads to the same structure of the proportionality test as the one outlined above. If one conceives of utility as being a constituent element of the concept of law,[46] then the three-partite requirements of proportionality can be portrayed as being inherent in the legal order.[47]

4.2.2.1.3 The Subtests as Basic Categories of Rational Decision-Making

According to *Hirschberg*, "ends"—and this term's linguistic variants such as effects, reasons for justification, rationale, telos, sense etc.—and "means"—causes etc.—are basic categories of thinking. Therefore, he argues, they underlie all sciences dealing with human acts and decisions.[48] This view is confirmed e.g. by writings in ethics, philosophy, political theory, and economics regarding the subtest of necessity, in particular.[49]

---

[43] Alexy (1994), pp. 71 ff.

[44] Wieacker (1979), p. 878.

[45] On the "*Ökonomiegebot*" cf. also the next section.

[46] Bydlinski (1991), pp. 133 and 486 ff; on the concept of law see also the comprehensive study by Bydlinski (1996).

[47] Cf. also Larenz (1979), p. 131.

[48] Hirschberg (1981), pp. 43 ff, 121 and 208.

[49] Brecht (1976), pp. 477 ff; Gäfgen (1974), pp. 102 ff (who refers to the "economic principle" ("*Ökonomiegebot*"), which can be understood as an expression of the test of necessity); on all of this cf. also Hirschberg (1981), pp. 43 ff; see also Perelman (1967), p. 100.

Similarly, the requirements of suitability and necessity can be regarded as an expression of the idea of Pareto-optimality.[50] Alternatively, the requirements of suitability and necessity can be inferred from the economic principle (*Ökonomiegebot*), according to which a given aim should be attained with minimal effort. This calls for the adoption of the "mildest means" among a set of suitable alternatives.[51]

In a related vein, the principle of proportionality with its three subtests has been characterized as an "axiom of rational behaviour".[52] Similarly, the three elements of suitability, necessity and proportionality in the narrow sense can be inferred from the definition of prudence (*prudentia*), pursuant to which prudence is the virtue according to which one chooses the means which are the most likely to promote, and the least burdensome to attain, one's goals.[53] These considerations underline that the principle of proportionality and its structure can plausibly be regarded as "valid"—in the sense of being acceptable or implicitly accepted—even beyond the realm of law.[54]

4.2.2.1.4 Interim Conclusion on the Status of Proportionality and Its Subtests

It ensues from the preceding considerations that the requirements of suitability, necessity and proportionality in the narrow sense represent maxims that should plausibly be applied in systematic-teleological interpretation, as they follow from the interplay between ends and means and the interrelation between rule and exception.

Hence, if one accepts on the basis of these and the related preceding considerations that these requirements apply with a high degree of plausibility in the interpretation of conflicting rights, resorting to the terminology of proportionality, balancing—and the disputed model of principles—may, as indicated, be quite illustrative. The fact that this is not indispensable, however, is shown by legal traditions which resolve similar problems in the terminology of "reasonableness" and similar concepts: in this context, it may be quite instructive to refer to the academic discussion on proportionality in the UK, where the standing of this principle is strongly disputed, since cases of competing rights are traditionally

[50] As explained by Alexy, if a means M_1 is not suitable to promote a given aim A_1, but causes costs for another relevant aim A_2, then both aims taken together prohibit the adoption of this means. If, on the other hand, there are two means M_1 and M_2 which are equally suitable to further a given aim A_1, but M_1 interferes more intensively with a second aim A_2, then the adoption of M_1 is prohibited by A_2. Cf. Alexy (2002), pp. 398–399.

[51] Cf. Gäfgen (1974), pp. 102–104.

[52] Hoffmann (1999), pp. 107–111.

[53] For this definition cf. Perelman (1967), p. 100.

[54] Cf. also Hirschberg (1981), pp. 43 ff, 121 and 208.

decided under the principle of "unreasonableness" there,[55] but where it has nonetheless been argued that the criteria of suitability, necessity and proportionality in the narrow sense are but *reasons* for a finding of "unreasonableness".[56]

As mentioned, some writers even regard the principle of proportionality as ensuing from the concept of law, as constituting a general principle of law, a general principle of international law, or even as "universal customary law".[57] Such views would provide an even firmer standing for the principle of proportionality and provide arguments a fortiori for the approach adopted here.

4.2.2.1.5 Proportionality, Good Faith and *abus de droit*

As indicated above, it follows from the approaches discussed that in case of two conflicting rights or interests, both of which are *legimitate*, teleological considerations imply that among available alternative means that means should be adopted which is *suitable* for reaching the aim, as well as *necessary* for, and *proportionate* to, the aim pursued.

Similar considerations apply to the principle of *abus de droit*, which is often regarded as the reverse side of the medal of the principle of good faith. The prohibition of *abus de droit* is sometimes understood as prohibiting an exercise of a right which is contrary to its "social function", or alternatively as the adoption of a means which is in excessive disproportion to the aim pursued.[58] The first alternative can be regarded as the prohibition of a means which does not contribute to the attainment of a legitimate aim and which is prohibited, therefore, as it is *unsuitable*; depending on the circumstances of the concrete case, it may also be regarded as not *necessary* and/or *disproportionate*. The second alternative *ex definitione* violates the principle of proportionality in its narrow sense. Hence, if one adopts this understanding of the principle of *abus de droit*, it fulfils functions analogous to the three requirements that are comprised by the principle of proportionality in the broad sense.

Moreover, the principle of *abus de droit* can be regarded as a proportionality test in the broad sense which is conducted with *greater deference*, such that more discretion is granted to the defendant in categorizing the means adopted as suitable,

---

[55] On the concepts of reasonableness and irrationality and their close relation to (or purported identity with) proportionality cf. Craig (1999), pp. 85 ff; Hoffmann (1999), pp. 107 ff.

[56] Craig (1999), p. 105 et passim; Hoffmann (1999), pp. 108 ff; pointing out that proportionality, being a standard of rationality as well, is therefore not "any different" from unreasonableness (Hoffmann (1999), p. 113), with the exception of the standard of review applied in certain cases (Craig (1999), pp. 96, 97 et passim; the varying degree of scrutiny under proportionality and unreasonableness is also pointed out by Jacobs (1999), p. 20; van Gerven (1999), p. 59; Tridimas (1999), p. 69).

[57] Cf. above, Sect. 4.2.2.

[58] Cf. e.g. Kiss (1992), pp. 4 ff; see also Kiss (1973), pp. 98 ff; from the perspective of EU law cf. Ottersbach (2001), pp. 33 ff; Meng (1984), p. 764.

necessary or proportionate. As just indicated, it is a question of expediency whether one brings the requirements of suitability, necessity and proportionality in its narrow sense together under the heading of a three-tier "principle of proportionality in the broad sense". If it is made clear that the principle of proportionality is to be understood this way, then the aim of simplification of argumentation may advocate such terminology. This does not exclude that other writers understand principles such as that of abuse of rights and reasonableness[59] in a similar way.

4.2.2.2 Further Remarks on the Requirements Comprised by Proportionality

Concerning the test of suitability, a central question is whether a means must be capable of guaranteeing the attainment of the legitimate purpose pursued with this means, or whether it is sufficient that the means contributes to promoting this aim. It has rightly been argued that this threshold should be set *low in general*, since otherwise a state or person pursuing ambitious legitimate aims may more easily be "punished" for not attaining his goal than someone who pursues a more moderate aim.[60] With regard to the "general exceptions" clause laid down in Article XX of the GATT, the WTO Appellate Body has similarly indicated that a measure is suitable, if it is capable of "simply making a contribution to" the promotion of a legitimate purpose.[61]

Turning to the subtest of necessity, a measure, as indicated above, is only to be regarded as necessary for the attainment of a legitimate end, if it is the least restrictive one from the perspective of the conflicting goal. This means that the side effects that are not relevant for the aim pursued need to be compared with the side effects of alternative means. This requirement involves two preliminary tests: First, it has to be ascertained whether there are (hypothetical) alternative means that are hypothetically *suitable* for promoting the aim pursued. Second, it has to be determined whether employing such alternatives are reasonable. This is reflected in

[59] Cf. e.g. Craig (1999), pp. 85 ff; Hoffmann (1999), pp. 107 ff.

[60] Cf. Hirschberg (1981), p. 51. In the Appellate Body's jurisprudence, there are indications that it might even be prepared to vary the threshold in correspondence to the importance of the legitimate aim pursued. This approach was first adopted in WTO Appellate Body report, *Korea – Measures Affecting Imports of Fresh, Chilled and Frozen Beef*, AB-2000-8, WT/DS 161 und 169/AB/R (*Korea – Beef*), 11 Dec 2000, para 161.

[61] Appellate Body report, *Korea – Beef*, para 161. Later rulings are discussed in Van den Bossche and Zdouc (2022), pp. 592 ff. This position converges remarkably with that of the German Constitutional Court, according to which "a means is suitable if it is *capable of contributing* to the promotion of the desired consequence" (BVerfGE 30, 292, quotation at 316: "ein Mittel ist geeignet, wenn mit seiner Hilfe der gewünschte Erfolg gefördert werden kann"). It apparently also converges with the stance traditionally taken by the ECJ (on this cf. Zeitler (2000), p. 122 with further references).

both GATT/WTO jurisprudence and academic writings on domestic law which hold that the alternative means must be "reasonably available".[62]

Importantly, since we are concerned with predictions in this context, namely the *hypothetical* suitability of *hypothetical* alternatives, there is considerable room for WTO panels to adjust the *standard of review* in concrete cases. A *strict* reading would have the effect that there is always only one single measure that is permissible in a given case, which has substantial implications for the scope of manoeuvre left to WTO Members, judicial decision-making and legitimacy. A more deferential application of the necessity test will grant more discretion to WTO Members regarding the questions of whether the measure at issue is to be *regarded* as suitable, whether alternative measures are to be *deemed* equally suitable to a sufficient degree, and whether the measure under scrutiny is to be *considered* to constitute the least restrictive means: if judicial review is undertaken with a decreased degree of scrutiny, a measure would e.g. be condemned only if it is clearly unsuitable (e.g. makes no or hardly any useful contribution to the stated legitimate policy goal); an alternative means would only be taken into consideration if it can be ascertained with a high degree of probability that its hypothetical suitability is equal to that of the means for which justification is sought; and, finally, such judicial deference may imply that a given measure may be justifiable not only if it is proven, with a very high degree of certainty, to be least restrictive, but also if it is likely to be less restrictive than alternative measures. A crucial question in this regard of course is which factors are determinant for the standard of review to be applied in a concrete context. These factors have to be determined through interpretation, taking into account explicit indications (such as the wording "it considers" in Article XXI) and implicit factors, the relevance of which may have to be ascertained through more extensive interpretive efforts such as the degree of discretion of the author of a rule (which relates to the problem of distribution of competences), the effect of the means adopted, the values protected, or a consistency test in the form of a comparison with the treatment of similar situations.

An important issue is the question as to whether one could forego one of the subtests of the proportionality analysis in certain legal contexts. Doing so does not appear plausible regarding the subtests of suitability and necessity: employing entirely unsuitable measures or excessively burdensome (i.e. unnecessary) means will normally be regarded as irrational, both as regards human conduct in general and the enactment of legal rules in particular. In other words, judicial control risks being reduced *ad absurdum*, if these two subtests were waived altogether. However, this could be different as respects the third subtest, i.e. the subtest of proportionality in the strict sense, in defined legal contexts: if one does not apply this third subtest after one has scrutinized the suitability and necessity of a measure, then it follows

[62] Cf. e.g. GATT panel report, *US – Section 337 of the Tariff Act of 1930*, report by the panel adopted on 7 November 1989 (L/6439—36S/345), para 5.26 ("all means that can *reasonably* be taken into account"); on German constitutional law cf. Hirschberg (1981), p. 59 ("alle *vernünftigerweise* in Betracht kommenden Mittel").

from such a limited system of judicial control that a lawmaking entity may, in such a restricted context, always impose the least restrictive measure that can be chosen from a set of available alternatives. This conception—which may seem counter-intuitive *prima facie*—appears to explain the approach taken in particular by the WTO Appellate Body under Article XX of the GATT as well as by the ECJ in similar constellations.[63]

4.2.3 Proportionality and the WTO Security Exceptions

As explained above, when interpreting Article XXI of the GATT, we are clearly concerned with a rule versus exception constellation. At the same time, Article XXI requires us to deal with the relationship between the ends pursued and the means adopted by a WTO Member.

As respects subparagraph (iii) of Article XXI(b), there is no need to have explicit recourse to the concept of "good faith", since the elements involved in the "normal" interpretive approach, which is called for under subparagraph (iii), can be regarded as concretized expressions of the principle of good faith anyway.

However, as indicated above, the WTO panel reports dealing with Article XXI(b) (iii) of the GATT (and Article 73(b)(iii) of the TRIPS Agreement) have expressly referred to the principle of good faith when interpreting the Chapeau. Yet, as has also been explained above, the principle of good faith underlies all treaty obligations. It is submitted here that this principle should be regarded as being concretized within the Chapeau by the proportionality principle for the following reasons. First, the wording of the Chapeau *explicitly* refers to the term "*necessary*... for the protection of...essential security interests". As pointed out above, the analysis of whether a measure is to be considered *necessary* requires determining whether the measure actually applied is least restrictive of trade, which presupposes determining whether

[63] As respects the ECJ's jurisprudence on the fundamental freedoms of the EU internal market, it has been noted that the ECJ almost never applies the subtest of proportionality in the strict sense, which means in principle that EU Member States may always pursue legitimate (non-economic) interests with a suitable measure that is least restrictive of trade. Turning to a provision like Article XX(b) or XX(d) of the GATT, foregoing the subtest of proportionality in the strict sense likewise means that WTO Members may pursue the goals mentioned in these provisions by adopting the least trade-restrictive measure that it suitable for promoting such goals. By contrast, if one argued that the subtest of proportionality in the strict sense ought to be applied under Article XX(b) or Article XX (d), then this would imply that even the least trade-restrictive means could be found to be illegal due to its effects on trade, which could lead to the result that in certain constellations the interest of free trade might outweigh legitimate non-economic goals that are pursued with a measure that constitutes the only suitable solution in a given case and/or which is the mildest means anyway. It should be stressed, however, that this question gives rise to "black-or-white answers" only *prima facie*: even if the subtest of proportionality in the strict sense were to be applied, this could be done with varying standards of review such that e.g. only blatantly disproportionate measures would be found not to be justifiable.

there are (hypothetical) alternative measures that are less restrictive of trade, but equally suitable. This in turn presupposes also determining the degree of *suitability* and the trade effects of the measure actually applied. Secondly, as has also been explained above, the same structure of analysis follows from the relationship between ends and means on the one hand, from the relationship between rule and exception on the other hand, and from the requirements of systematic-teleological interpretation. Thirdly, the largely analogous structure in the "general exceptions" clause of Article XX of the GATT has led WTO adjudicating bodies to adopt a similar interpretive approach.[64]

A precondition for the analysis of the suitability and necessity both of the measure employed and hypothetical alternatives is the determination of the *aim* pursued. In a comparative perspective, it is noteworthy that WTO dispute settlement practice under the "general exceptions" clause of Article XX of the GATT appears to be prepared to adopt a broad interpretation of relevant policy goals.[65] Moreover, WTO panels have repeatedly underlined that it is not their task under Article XX "to examine generally the desirability or necessity" of the aims of a defending WTO Member's measures.[66] Furthermore, panels and the Appellate Body have expressly held that establishing the appropriate level of protection of a legitimate policy goal like public security in Article XX "is a *prerogative* of the Member concerned and not of panels or the Appellate Body" in principle.[67] The approach adopted by the panel

---

[64] Cf. Van den Bossche and Zdouc (2022), pp. 592 ff.

[65] Cf. Vranes (2009), pp. 263–264; Weiß et al. (2022), p. 200.

[66] Cf. e.g. the Panel Report, *United States – Standards for Reformulated and Conventional Gasoline*, WT/DS2/R, adopted 20 May 1996, as modified by Appellate Body Report, United States – Standards for Reformulated and Conventional Gasoline, WT/DS2/AB/R, adopted 20 May 1996, DSR 1996:I, 3, 29 (*US – Gasoline*), para. 7.1; similarly, the panel in *United States – Restrictions on Imports of Tuna*, (unadopted) DS21/R—BISD 39S/155, 3 September 1991 (*US – Tuna I*), para. 5.32 held that the conditions set out in Article XX(g) do not relate to the conservation policies pursued by a contracting party, but merely to the measures adopted in pursuit of these goals. Nonetheless, several decisions in fact have implicitly or explicitly reviewed the legitimacy of the policy goal pursued by determining whether a stated policy falls within one of the categories set out in the individual paragraphs of Art. XX and whether the value protected by these provisions is actually at risk in the case at issue (cf. Vranes (2009), pp. 264–265 with further references).

[67] Cf. the Appellate Body Report, *European Communities – Measures Affecting Asbestos and Asbestos-Containing Products*, WT/DS135/AB/R, adopted 5 April 2001, DSR 2001:VII, 3243 (*EC – Asbestos*), para. 199; the quotation is taken from para 199 the Appellate Body Report, Australia – Measures Affecting Importation of Salmon, WT/DS18/AB/R, adopted 6 November 1998, DSR 1998:VIII, p. 3327 that was issued under the SPS Agreement, which according to its preamble elaborates the rules of Art. XX(b) GATT; see also Appellate Body Report, *Korea – Beef*, para 176 ("It is not open to doubt that Members of the WTO have the right to determine for themselves the level of enforcement of their WTO-consistent laws and regulations"); panel report, *United States – Section 337*, para. 5.26 ("The Panel wished to make it clear that this [the obligation to choose a reasonably available GATT-consistent or less inconsistent measure] does not mean that a contracting party could be asked to change its substantive patent law or its desired *level of enforcement* of that law"). The Appellate Body has nonetheless questioned the level of protection adopted by WTO Members in at least two ways. First, in the seminal *Korea – Beef* case, the

in *Russia – Transit* under Article XXI is clearly in line with this approach, as it reasoned that "it is left, in general, to every Member to define what it considers to be its essential security interests".[68]

As indicated above, the proportionality analysis required under the Chapeau next calls for an assessment of the suitability of the measure adopted by the WTO Member invoking Article XXI(b)(iii). The crucial question under the subtest of suitability, too, is establishing the legally appropriate standard of review. As expounded above, deference is *prima facie* appropriate under this analytical step.[69] In the concrete context of the Chapeau, this applies *a fortiori* in view of the phrase "it considers" in the Chapeau as well as the systematic and teleological argument just mentioned that this analysis relates to a WTO Member's quintessential interests. The "not implausible" standard adopted by the panel in *Russia – Transit* arguably is clearly in line with this interpretation of the Chapeau; it is also in line with WTO Appellate Body jurisprudence under Article XX of the GATT, which has likewise decreased the degree of scrutiny in cases where a WTO Member's vital interests are at stake.[70]

The next analytical step calls for an analysis of the necessity of the measure actually applied, which, as indicated, requires determining whether there are less trade restrictive measures that appear equally suitable. As has also been stated above, since the necessity test is concerned with predictions regarding the trade effects of hypothetical alternatives, whose (hypothetical) suitability needs to be estimated, there *prima facie* is considerable space for judges to determine the standard of review to be applied under the tests of suitability and necessity, the appropriate degree of scrutiny having to be ascertained through legal interpretation. In the context of the Chapeau of Article XXI(b)(iii), there are clear indications that WTO panels are called upon to apply a high degree of deference. One indication consists in particular in the explicit wording "it considers". A second indication derives from functional considerations (i.e. the relationship between states and the international judicature), namely the fact that the necessity test *in concreto* is concerned with vital state interests, which have rightly been regarded by the panel in *Russia – Transit* as

---

Appellate Body did not accept the defendant's *stated* level of protection of its policy goal, but re-adjusted it by drawing an "inverse" inference from the measure to the presumable level of protection against which the suitability of less restrictive alternatives was then assessed (The Appellate Body held: "[w]e *think it unlikely* that Korea intended to establish a *level of protection* that totally eliminates fraud with respect to the origin of beef (domestic or foreign) sold by retailers. The total elimination of fraud would probably require a total ban of imports. Consequently, we assume that in effect Korea intended to reduce considerably the number of cases of fraud occurring with respect to the origin of beef sold by retailers" (Appellate Body Report, *Korea – Beef*, para. 178 (italics added)); on this see Vranes (2009), p. 265; Weiß et al. (2022), p. 200). Second, the presumable level of protection pursued under Article XX has also been established by WTO adjudicating bodies themselves, when the defendant had *not clearly stated* the degree of protection sought (cf. Vranes (2009), pp. 265 ff).

[68] Panel report, *Russia – Transit*, para 7.131 (italics added); on this see above, Sect. 3.4.4.1.

[69] See above, Sect. 3.4.4.1.

[70] Vranes (2009), pp. 271 ff.

relating to the "quintessential functions of a state"[71] that should not be subjected to strict scrutiny for reasons of judicial deference. As noted above, the panel in *Russia – Transit* surprisingly declined to analyze the issue of the necessity of the measure employed. As pointed out, this is clearly problematic, as foregoing the necessity test altogether does not correspond to the explicit wording of the Chapeau and risks undermining the rationality analysis, which is a main function of the necessity test.[72] As has rightly been argued by the EU in the *US – Steel* dispute, the wording "it considers necessary" evidently calls for a necessity analysis, albeit one to be applied with considerable deference.[73]

The last subtest within a proportionality analysis theoretically is the test of proportionality in the strict sense. As has been explained in the preceding section, this subtest can arguably be foregone on the basis of indications that this subtest is not called for in clearly defined legal contexts. As already explained above, applying this subtest would lead to the result that even a measure which is suitable and least trade restrictive could be regarded as being prohibited. It is submitted that there are no indications in the Chapeau of Article XXI(b)(iii) calling for such an analysis, which would unduly restrict the autonomy of WTO Members, when their essential security interests are at stake.

4.2.4 Interim Conclusions on Article XXI and Proportionality

In sum, it has been argued in the preceding analysis that while the principle of good faith underlies all treaty obligations, it is concretized in the context of the Chapeau of Article XXI(b) by a proportionality analysis, which encompasses an assessment of the suitability and necessity of the measures applied by the WTO Member invoking Article XXI(b)(iii). Such an analysis is called for by the wording of the Chapeau of Article XXI(b), which explicitly requires a necessity test, and the structure of the Chapeau, which is concerned with an analysis of ends and means, which requires an analysis of the suitability and necessity of the means employed. Such an analysis is also requisite for methodological reasons, since systematic-teleological interpretation in a rule versus exception constellation necessitates an examination of the suitability and necessity of the actions taken.

Hence, as has rightly been pointed out in the literature, Article XXI(b)(iii) as applied in the panel reports discussed above channels the relationship between economic and security concerns through an argumentative framework that is structured by questions of suitability and necessity, the essentiality of the goals pursued,

---

[71] See above, Sect. 3.4.4.1.

[72] Cf. above, Sects. 4.2.2.1 and 4.2.2.2.

[73] See also the EU statement in the *US – Steel* dispute (European Union, Opening Oral Statement, *United States – Certain Measures on Steel and Aluminium Products*, DS548, Geneva, 4 November 2019, paras 90, 122).

an elaboration of the categories of security interests that can be invoked under this provision, and explanations of the discretionary space available for WTO Members under the WTO security exceptions.[74]

Furthermore, as has also been submitted, the proportionality analysis applied by these panel reports has indeed narrowed the distance between the GATT's "general exceptions" clause (Article XX) and its "security exception" clause (and Article XXI), since roughly the same scrutiny has been applied under both exception clauses.[75]

Finally, while it has been argued that the WTO panels' reasoning amounts to "strategic ambiguity", which may be "the best" that the WTO has to offer,[76] it has been submitted here that this approach is not merely "strategic", but requisite for reasons of law and legal methodology.

References

Akande D, Williams S (2003) International adjudication on national security issues: what role for the WTO? Virginia J Int Law 43:365–404

Alexy R (1994) Theorie der Grundrechte. Suhrkamp, Frankfurt aM

Alexy R (2002) A theory of constitutional rights. Oxford University Press, Oxford

Barak A (2012) Proportionality. Cambridge University Presse, Cambridge

Bleckmann A (1995) Allgemeine Staats- und Völkerrechtslehre. Heymann, Köln

Bockslaff K (1987) Das völkerrechtliche Interventionsverbot als Schranke außenpolitisch motivierter Handelsbeschränkungen. Duncker & Humblot, Berlin

Brecht A (1976) Politische Theorie. Die Grundlagen politischen Denkens im 20. Jahrhundert. Mohr, Tübingen

Bydlinski F (1991) Juristische Methodenlehre und Rechtsbegriff. Springer, Wien

Bydlinski F (1996) System und Prinzipien des Privatrechts. Springer, Wien

Cohen HG (2020) Nations and markets. J Int Econ Law 23:793–815

Cohen-Eliya M, Porat I (2010) American balancing and German proportionality: the historical origins. Int J Constitutional Law 8(2):263–286

Craig P (1999) Unreasonableness and proportionality in UK law. In: Ellis E (ed) The principle of proportionality in the laws of Europe. Hart, Oxford, pp 85–106

Delbrück J (1984) Proportionality. In: Bernhardt R (ed) Encyclopedia of public international law, vol 7. North-Holland Pub. Co, Amsterdam, p 396

Delbrück J (1997) Proportionality. In: Bernhardt R (ed) Encyclopedia of public international law, vol III. North-Holland Pub. Co, Amsterdam, p 1140

Dicke DC (1978) Die Intervention mit wirtschaftlichen Mitteln im Völkerrecht. Nomos, Baden-Baden

Ellis E (1999) The principle of proportionality in the laws of Europe. Hart, Oxford

Gäfgen G (1974) Theorie der wirtschaftlichen Entscheidung, 3rd edn. Mohr (Paul Siebeck), Tübingen

Gladysz J (2021) The national security exception in WTO law: emerging jurisprudence and future direction. Georgetown J Int Law 52:835–861

[74] Cohen (2020), pp. 799 and 812.

[75] Heath (2020), pp. 256 ff.

[76] Gladysz (2021), p. 861.

Hahn MJ (1991) Vital interests and the law of the GATT: an analysis of GATT’s security exception. Mich J Int Law 12(3):558–620
Heath JB (2020) Trade and security among the ruins. Duke J Comp Int Law 30:223–266
Hilf M, Puth S (2002) The principle of proportionality on its way into WTO/GATT law. In: von Bogdandy A, Mavroidis PC, Mény Y (eds) European integration and international co-ordination, studies in transnational economic law in honour of Claus-Dieter Ehlermann. Kluwer Law International, The Hague, pp 199–218
Hirschberg L (1981) Der Grundsatz der Verhältnismäßigkeit. Schwartz, Göttingen
Hoffmann L (1999) The influence of the principle of proportionality upon UK law. In: Ellis E (ed) The principle of proportionality in the laws of Europe. Hart, Oxford, pp 107–116
Holoubek M (1995) Zur Begründung des Verhältnismäßigkeitsgrundsatzes – verwaltungs-, verfassungs- und gemeinschaftsrechtliche Aspekte. In: Griller S et al (eds) Grundfragen und aktuelle Probleme des öffentlichen Rechts. Festschrift für Heinz Peter Rill zum 60. Geburtstag. Orac, Vienna, pp 97–130
Jacobs FG (1999) Recent developments in the principle of proportionality in European community law. In: Ellis E (ed) The principle of proportionality in the laws of Europe. Hart, Oxford, pp 1–22
Jans JH (2000) Proportionality revisited. Leg Issues Econ Integr 27:239–265
Jenks CW (1958) The common law of mankind. Frederick A. Praeger, New York
Kiss A (1973) Comments on W Rudolf, Territoriale Grenzen der staatlichen Rechtsetzung. Berichte der Detschen Gesellschaft für Völkerrecht 11:98–101
Kiss A (1992) Abuse of rights. In: Bernhardt R (ed) Encyclopedia of public international law, vol I. North-Holland Pub. Co, Amsterdam, p 4
Klemm UD (1981) Continental shelf arbitration. In: Bernhardt R (ed) Encyclopedia of public international law, vol II. North-Holland Pub. Co, Amsterdam, p 58
Koskenniemi M (1990) The politics of international law. Eur J Int Law 1:4–32
Krugmann M (2004) Der Grundsatz der Verhältnismäßigkeit im Völkerrecht. Duncker & Humblot, Berlin
Larenz K (1979) Richtiges Recht. Grundzüge einer Rechtsethik. Beck, München
Mantilla Blanco S, Pehl A (2020) National security exceptions in international trade and investment agreements. Justiciability and standards of review. Springer, Cham
Mathews J, Stone Sweet A (2011) All things in proportion? American rights review and the problem of balancing. Emory Law J 60:797–875
Medicus D (1992) Der Grundsatz der Verhältnismäßigkeit im Privatrecht. Archiv für die civilistische Praxis 192:35–70
Meng W (1984) Völkerrechtliche Zulässigkeit und Grenzen wirtschaftsverwaltungsrechtlicher Hoheitsakte mit Auslandswirkung. Zeitschrift für ausländisches öffentliches Recht und Völkerrecht 44:676–783
Mosler H (1976) Völkerrecht als Rechtsordnung. Zeitschrift für ausländisches öffentliches Recht und Völkerrecht 36:6–49
Neumann J, Türk E (2003) Necessity revisited: proportionality in World Trade Organization law after Korea—Beef, EC—Asbestos and EC—Sardines. J World Trade 37(1):199–233
Ottersbach K (2001) Rechtsmißbrauch bei den Grundfreiheiten des Europäischen Binnenmarktes. Nomos, Baden-Baden
Ottmann H (1980) Maß. In: Ritter J, Gründer K (eds) Historisches Wörterbuch der Philosophie, vol V. Schwabe, Basel, pp 808–809
Perelman CH (1967) Über die Gerechtigkeit. Beck, München
Röhl KF, Röhl HC (2008) Allgemeine Rechtslehre, 3rd edn. Heymann, Köln
Schill S, Briese R (2009) “If the state considers”: self-judging clauses in international dispute settlement. In: von Bogdandy A, Wolfrum R (eds) Max Planck Yearbook of United Nations Law, vol 13, pp 61–140
Schloemann HL, Ohlhoff S (1999) Constitutionalization and dispute settlement in the WTO: national security as an issue of competence. Am J Int Law 93:424–451

Stone Sweet A, Mathews J (2008) Proportionality balancing and global constitutionalism. Columbia J Trans Law 47:72–164

Tridimas T (1999) Proportionality in European community law: searching for the appropriate standard of scrutiny. In: Ellis E (ed) The principle of proportionality in the laws of Europe. Hart, Oxford, pp 83–101

Van den Bossche P, Akpofure S (2020) The use and abuse of the national security exception under Article XXI(b)(iii) of the GATT 1994. WTI working paper no. 03/2020. https://www.wti.org/research/publications/1299/the-use-and-abuse-of-the-national-security-exception-under-article-xxibiii-of-the-gatt-1994. Accessed 4 Jan 2023

Van den Bossche P, Zdouc W (2022) The law and policy of the World Trade Organization, 5th edn. Cambridge University Press, Cambridge

van Gerven W (1999) The effect of proportionality on the actions of Member States of the European community: national viewpoints from continental Europe. In: Ellis E (ed) The principle of proportionality in the laws of Europe. Hart, Oxford, pp 37–64

Vranes E (2009) Trade and the environment. Fundamental issues in international law, WTO law, and legal theory. Oxford University Press, Oxford

Vranes E (2017) Vom "rechten Maß" zum globalen Rechtsgrundsatz? Schlaglichter in der Entwicklung des Verhältnismäßigkeitsgrundsatzes. In: Herzig G, Klamert M, Palmstorfer R, Puff R, Weismann P (eds) Europarecht und Rechtstheorie. Verlag Österreich, Vienna, pp 99–136

Weiß W, Ohler C, Bungenberg M (2022) Welthandelsrecht, 3rd edn. Beck, Munich

Wieacker F (1979) Geschichtliche Wurzeln des Prinzips der verhältnismäßigen Rechtsanwendung. In: Lutter M (ed) Festschrift für Robert Fischer, pp 867–882

Zeitler HE (2000) Einseitige Handelsbeschränkungen zum Schutz extraterritorialer Rechtsgüter. Nomos, Baden-Baden

Chapter 5
Concluding Remarks

This section sets out some of the key conclusions of this study. It does so in a very condensed manner, given that more elaborate interim conclusions have been stated at the end of the main chapters (Chaps. 3 and 4).

On a (geo-)political level, the invocation of the GATT and TRIPS security exceptions by Russia, Saudi-Arabia and the US in WTO proceedings has rightly been regarded as a turning point in international economic relations: there is a danger that the floodgates have been opened to some extent, incurring the risk that these once "dormant" clauses will be used more often in political and legal disputes that are increasingly removed from armed conflicts.[1]

This development is connected with trends in national and international politics that conceive of national security in a considerably broader sense than in the past. Hence, there is a growing risk that the WTO security exceptions will be instrumentalized to contest the rules-based international trading system and international governance structures of the post-World War II era.[2]

An additional future challenge for the international economic order could be "good-faith but novel" national security claims relating to concerns such as climate change, pandemics, cybercrime, terrorism, infrastructure, threats to industry, the media and other areas.[3] These concerns, which have recently become reasons for screening foreign investments in several countries,[4] may become relevant in trade relations as well. As has been pointed out, such novel security interests could be subjected to a higher burden of argumentation, in line with the "sliding scale"

---

[1] A case in point e.g. is an announcement by China in December 2022 that it intends to bring a complaint before the WTO in order to challenge US export controls on semiconductors, which were justified by the US as being required for national security reasons. Cf. Fortnam (2022).

[2] Reinsch (2022).

[3] Heath (2020a), pp. 1020 ff (quotation at 1020).

[4] Cf. e.g. Bohnert (2022), pp. 10 ff.

E. Vranes, *WTO Security Exceptions in Practice and Scholarship*, SpringerBriefs in Law, https://doi.org/10.1007/978-3-031-36702-1_5

approach adopted by the panel in *Russia – Transit* in order to adjust the burden of argumentation, when a WTO Member invokes essential security interests.[5]

On the level of WTO judicial proceedings, the panel reports in *Russia – Transit* and *Saudi Arabia – IPRs* as well as the 2022 *US – Steel* panel reports have clarified the cardinal issue that disputes involving the WTO security exceptions come under the jurisdiction of WTO panels and are justiciable. However, the problem remains that there are still divergences between these reports regarding the interpretation of principal concepts in the security exceptions and the pertinent standards of review. It is conspicuous, moreover, that the "sliding scale approach," which had been introduced in *Russia – Transit*, has not been applied in this manner by the panel in *Saudi Arabia – IPRs*. Furthermore, it is rather astonishing that the 2022 *US – Steel* panel reports have refrained from referring to the reasoning in the preceding reports.

The considerable tension that exists between national security concerns and international scrutiny of treaty-based security exceptions is illustrated by recent developments outside the WTO, where several states have started to negotiate security exceptions that appear to preclude control by international dispute settlement bodies altogether.[6]

On the level of legal methodology, it has been argued that there is no need to draw analogies with national law in order to "operationalize" the review of the principle of good faith that has been resorted to in the panel reports dealing the WTO security exceptions. By contrast, it has been submitted in this study that the principle of good faith, which underlies all treaty obligations, should be regarded as being concretized, for reasons of law and legal methodology, in the case of the WTO security exceptions by a proportionality test that encompasses the scrutiny of the suitability and necessity of the trade measures taken, which has to be conducted with considerably increased deference.

Finally, as has been explained by way of introduction, the security exceptions of the GATT, GATS and TRIPS Agreements have been regarded as the "box of Pandora" of WTO law. It is submitted that through the approach taken in the panel reports issued so far, this box has largely been kept closed. How firmly locked it is, however, depends not least on the degree of discretion accorded to WTO Members in future cases.

---

[5] Heath (2020a), pp. 1075 ff; Heath (2020b), pp. 261 ff.

[6] Cf. the Free Trade Agreement between the US and Korea, Chapter 23 (Exceptions), fn 2, which states "if a Party invokes Article 23.2 in an arbitral proceeding initiated under Chapter Eleven (Investment) or Chapter Twenty-Two (Institutional Provisions and Dispute Settlement), the tribunal or panel hearing the matter shall find that the exception applies" (on this cf. also the European Union, Opening Oral Statement, *United States – Certain Measures on Steel and Aluminium Products*, DS548, Geneva, 4 November 2019, para 85); cf. also Schill and Vidigal (2021), p. 506, who also refer to the Comprehensive Economic Cooperation Agreement between India and Singapore as a further example; see also Lester (2021) referring to Article 12.14 of the Regional Comprehensive Economic Partnership Agreement.

References

Bohnert S (2022) EU investment screening: a roadblock in a one-way street? In: Winner M (ed) Kontrolle ausländischer Direktinvestitionen in Mittel- und Osteuropa. Nomos, facultas, Vienna

Fortnam B (2022) China to challenge U.S. semiconductor export controls at WTO. Inside US Trade 40(50), 16 December 2022

Heath JB (2020a) The new national security challenge to the economic order. Yale Law J 129: 1020–1098

Heath JB (2020b) Trade and security among the ruins. Duke J Comp Int Law 30:223–266

Lester S (2021) RCEP's airtight data localization security exception. International Economic Law and Policy Blog, 26 September 2021. https://ielp.worldtradelaw.net/2021/09/rceps-airtight-data-localization-security-exception.html. Accessed 12 Jan 2023

Reinsch WA (2022) The view from under the bus. Center for Strategic and International Studies, 12 December 2022. https://www.csis.org/analysis/view-under-bus. Accessed 11 Jan 2023

Schill S, Vidigal G (2021) National security, private actors, and political risk: judicial and non-judicial responses. J World Invest Trade 22:503–508

Table of Cases

GATT 1947 and WTO Disputes and Panel Reports

Russia – Measures Concerning Traffic in Transit, WT/DS512/R and Add.1, adopted 26 April 2019, DSR 2019:VIII, 4301 (*Russia – Transit*)

Saudi Arabia – Measures Concerning the Protection of Intellectual Property Rights, WT/DS567/R and Add.1, circulated to WTO Members on 16 June 2020, dispute terminated while appeal pending (*Saudi Arabia – IPRs*)

United States – Restrictions on Imports of Tuna, (unadopted) DS21/R – BISD 39S/155, 3 September 1991 (*US – Tuna I*).

United States – Standards for Reformulated and Conventional Gasoline, WT/DS2/R, adopted 20 May 1996, as modified by Appellate Body Report WT/DS2/AB/R, DSR 1996:I, 29 (*US – Gasoline*)

United States – Certain Measures on Steel and Aluminium Products, WT/DS550/R, 11 July 2019, mutually agreed solution reported (complaint by Canada)

United States – Certain Measures on Steel and Aluminium Products, WT/DS544/R, Add.1 and Suppl.1, circulated to WTO Members 9 December 2022 (*US – Steel (China)*)

United States – Certain Measures on Steel and Aluminium Products, WT/DS551/R, 11 July 2019, mutually agreed solution reported (complaint by Mexico)

United States – Certain Measures on Steel and Aluminium Products, WT/DS552/R, Add.1 and Suppl.1, circulated to WTO Members 9 December 2022 (*US – Steel (Norway)*)

United States – Certain Measures on Steel and Aluminium Products, WT/DS556/R, Add.1 and Suppl.1, circulated to WTO Members 9 December 2022 (*US – Steel (Switzerland)*)

United States – Certain Measures on Steel and Aluminium Products, WT/DS564/R, Add.1 and Suppl.1, circulated to WTO Members 9 December 2022 (*US – Steel (Turkey)*)

E. Vranes, *WTO Security Exceptions in Practice and Scholarship*, SpringerBriefs in Law, https://doi.org/10.1007/978-3-031-36702-1

United States – Certain Measures on Steel and Aluminium Products, WT/DS548 (Mutually Agreed Solution notified on 20 January 2022)
United States – Certain Measures on Steel and Aluminium Products, WT/DS547 (complaint by India, panel composed on 25 January 2019)
United States – Certain Measures on Steel and Aluminium Products, WT/DS554 (complaint by Russia, panel composed on 25 January 2019)

WTO Appellate Body Reports

Australia – Measures Affecting Importation of Salmon, WT/DS18/AB/R, adopted 6 November 1998, DSR 1998:VIII, 3327 (*Australia – Salmon*)
European Communities – Measures Affecting Asbestos and Asbestos- Containing Products, WT/DS135/AB/R, adopted 5 April 2001, DSR 2001:VII, 3243 (*EC – Asbestos*)
Korea – Measures Affecting Imports of Fresh, Chilled and Frozen Beef, WT/DS161/AB/R, WT/DS169/AB/R, adopted 10 January 2001, DSR 2001:I, 5 (*Korea – Beef*)
United States – Standards for Reformulated and Conventional Gasoline, WT/DS2/AB/R, adopted 20 May 1996, DSR 1996:I, 3 (*US – Gasoline*)
United States – Import Prohibition of Certain Shrimp and Shrimp Products, WT/DS58/AB/R, adopted 6 November 1998, DSR 1998:VII, 2755 (*US – Shrimp*)
United States – Tax Treatment for "Foreign Sales Corporations", WT/DS108/AB/R, adopted 20 March 2000, DSR 2000:III, 1619 (*US – FSC*)

The manufacturer's authorised representative in the EU is Springer Nature Customer Service Centre GmbH, Europaplatz 3, 69115 Heidelberg, Germany. If you have any concerns regarding our products, please contact ProductSafety@springernature.com

Printed and bound by CPI Group (UK) Ltd, Croydon, CR0 4YY
01/10/2026
02225839-0002